FIELD

FIELD SECURITY

Very Ordinary Intelligence

by

Tony Mains

Published by
Picton Publishing (Chippenham) Ltd
England

Field Security
by
Tony Mains
first published in 1992 by
Picton Publishing (Chippenham) Ltd.
Queensbridge Cottages
Patterdown
Chippenham
Wiltshire SN15 2NS

Copyright © T. Mains 1992

Represented to the Home Book Trade by
MSR Books
1 Polhill Drive
Walderslade
Chatham, Kent
ME5 9PN

ISBN 0 11 948251 57 3

*Typeset and Printed in Great Britain by
Hobbs the Printers of Southampton*

To
my wife 'Paul'

Contents

Acknowledgements and Thanks

First of all my thanks go to the Chief of the General Staff, General Sir John Chapple for writing the Foreword. I have been associated with him for many years mainly in connection with the Gurkha Museum, and I am grateful for his interest and help. Next I must mention those who have so kindly read all or part of the manuscript — namely General 'Monty' Palit, and Harold Warren both of whom served at one time or another in the 9th Gurkhas and Patric Emerson, the Hon Secretary of the Indian Army Association.

The Curators of the Intelligence Corps and Gurkha Museums have kindly made material available for illustrations.

Most of all my grateful thanks must go to my wife, 'Paul', who besides bullying me into writing this book, read it in manuscript and was invaluable in correcting my English and generally giving the work a polish.

Tony Mains

Foreword

by

General Sir John Chapple GCB CBE ADC Gen.

FIELD Security is an important aspect of Military Intelligence, which was developed during the Second World War, by the end of which time all the principles and procedures still in use today had been worked out and worked up to a high state of effectiveness.

The early beginnings of Field Security were fraught with difficulty and Tony Mains' story has an importance in its own right since he could well be described as the father of the Indian Field Security service. He raised the first Composite Indian Field Security Sections in Iraq in 1941, and these were taken as the model for the later sections of the newly formed Indian Intelligence Corps.

Tony Mains' qualifications were particularly appropriate for the job. He had passed out top of a Command Intelligence Course in 1939 and had been an Instructor at the new Intelligence School in 1941.

His later service, partly recounted in his book 'Retreat from Burma' covered a wide range of Intelligence appointments, starting with Chief Security Officer, Iraq Force, then for Burma Army during the Retreat, then in Assam and XIV Army. The present book covers this service and finally his tour in Central Command, India in 1946.

The underlining theme is the heavy burden of responsibility carried by relatively junior Officers with little or no specialist training; this, however, was not so unusual in the Indian Army, where Second Lieutenants were expected to be able to command Companies.

This books also brings out the muddle and confusion which was often apparent in those theatres of war, and it provides a valuable insight of both how not to do it, and how to do it when proper integration of intelligence and field security is achieved.

It therefore provides a useful inside view of a little recorded aspect of war.

Prologue

INTELLIGENCE — an emotive word bringing to mind glamorous spies, internationally renowned Hotels, the Orient Express and other trappings beloved of the thriller writers. In practice Intelligence merely means trying to find out about your enemy — Espionage, or preventing your enemy finding out about you — Counter Espionage or Security as it became known later.

The Intelligence Branch of the British Army, in the nineteenth century was found in the Department of the Quartermaster General, but on the formation of the General Staff in 1904, it became one of its Directorates, the Directorate of Military Intelligence (MI) in the War Office and Army Headquarters, India, or General Staff (Intelligence) in lower formations. The terms 'MI 5' for the present Security service and 'MI 6' for the Secret Intelligence Service show their origins.

Much of the work of GS (I) was of a necessary but routine nature, far removed from any glamour; what glamour there was, was found in a number of ancilliary agencies, such as the Special Operations Executive, and on the Eastern Front, Force 136, 'V' Force and 'Z' Force, agencies formed in World War II to penetrate far behind the enemy lines or into enemy controlled territory to gain intelligence or to sabotage the enemy's war effort.

I spent five years during or immediately after World War II in GS (Ib), the Counter Espionage or Security section of GS (I); this amounted to about one quarter of my total service with the old Indian Army. I rose to be the Chief Intelligence Officer of an Army Command — Central Command, India, dealing with an area the size of France and Benelux put together, but I was almost entirely self taught, my total time spent in formal instruction being ten days.

CHAPTER ONE

Command Intelligence Course and Intelligence School

I WAS commissioned into the Indian Army in 1934 and joined the 2nd Battalion of the 9th Gurkha Rifles in the following year. By 1939, I had five years service and, as peace time routine could be somewhat boring, I began to look about for a change. Many Officers of this length of service would go off 'scallywagging' to get a break from routine. This could be secondment to one of the Frontier Corps on the North West Frontier or the para military Assam Rifles in the North East or the Burma Frontier Force. I was greatly impressed, however, by the stories told by our Adjutant of his service on the North West Frontier seconded to the RAF as an Air Intelligence Liaison Officer, so I decided that this would be what I would try for.

The qualification for such a post was attendance at and a recommendation from a Command Intelligence Course. A snag arose in that students were supposed to have seven years service and I had only five; I applied, however, and to my surprise was accepted. A further snag arose when the date and venue of the course was announced; it was to start in Bareilly on a Monday in early March, but on the Tuesday, I was to report at Delhi to take the second part of my promotion examination for Captain. I had already passed the first part, so my Commanding Officer was adamant that this was the more important, while on the other hand my selection for the course had been wangled by a Staff Officer at District Headquarters, and he would not be pleased if I passed up on his efforts. Enquiries were made, the upshot of which were that if I could get to Bareilly in time to start work on Thursday morning, I would be accepted.

I cannot say that either the Course or my fellow students were very inspiring. Intelligence was very much of a backwater at that time. The Course tried to squeeze too much into too short a time — Military Intelligence in War, Air Photo Interpretation, Internal Security, Indian Intelligence, all in twelve working days. I can remember one exercise, probably as I was the Syndicate Leader; we were sent off to prepare an Intelligence Report on a nearby District, Budaon, and the Chief Instructor had decreed that none of the District Staff should speak to us in English. They were all Indians and they obeyed their instructions to the letter. All the others of my Syndicate were British Service Officers, who had little or no knowledge of Urdu, so the bulk of the work fell on me. I was rewarded some six years later, when as Chief Intelligence Officer of Central Command, I found our report was still the standard work on the District.

My course result exceeded all my expections; I passed out top and was recommended for a wide range of Intelligence appointments, ranging from a General Staff officer 3rd Grade Intelligence (GSO III(I)) in war, through an Air Intelligence Liason Officer to Indian Political Intelligence. My preference had veered away from being an IALO to Civil Intelligence and appointment as a 'Military Intelligence Officer' (MIO) with the Intelligence Bureau of the Government of India. The Intelligence Bureau was India's MI5 and MI6 combined and MIOs were seconded to the Civil Police in difficult or disturbed areas, where they acted as Field Agents of the IB and as a liaison between the Military and the Police to which end they were granted the rank of Additional Superintendent of Police. The final remarks on my report read 'He desires training for employment as an MIO and should be attached to Army HQ for that purpose'. So it appeared that I had got what I wanted, or had I?

My Commanding Officer did not approve of my desire to leave the Regiment. This may have been because he had come to us from the 5th Gurkhas; a Regiment notorious for its dislike of Officers who went on to the Staff or into Extra Regimental Employment. Additionally I was substantive Quartermaster (Indian units did not have professional QMs) and would probably go up to Adjutant in a few months time.

All was put into abeyance as I went off to England on two months leave. Two offers of civil employment were made while I was away — the first as MIO at Ranchi in Bihar, and the other as Second in Command of the newly raised Crown Representative's Police at Neemuch in Rajputana. The CRP was a Government of India Force raised to support small Native States, who had no proper forces to deal with serious disorder and to keep communications open. My CO had pulled out all the stops with District and Brigade HQs, saying I was indispensable to the Battalion as war now appeared imminent, Modern readers may find it odd that I was 'offered' these appointments, rather than being ordered to them; the reason was that an Officer could not be ordered to take up an appointment with the civil Government against his will.

Shortly after the outbreak of war, the battalion was ordered to do a crash move to Nowshera to replace the 1st Dorsets, who had gone to the Middle East, and later to move on to Landi Kotal in the Khyber Pass to relieve the 1st South Wales Borderers; this was part of a new idea of garrisoning the North West Frontier, whereby Gurkha battalions would replace British. The move was at such short notice that the most senior Officer present and available was myself, a Lieutenant of five years service; so I commanded the battalion during the move. Officers of the present British Army treat this with some disbelief, but it was in no way extraordinary in the Indian Army, where you were expected to command a Company as a 2/Lieutenant, within weeks of your arrival.

I was at Landi Kotal during the winter of 1939–40, first as Quartermaster and then as Adjutant, and any Intelligence appointment seemed very far away, but Army HQ had not forgotten me. India did not mobilise in 1939, nor did she start the expansion of her Army until after the fall of France, but she was committed to three overseas reinforcements. Two involved the reinforcement of the Middle East and Malaya, but the third was one which many people do not know of even today: this was the setting up of a Line of Communication HQ, with the necessary transportation and other units to operate a road and rail link between Basra in Iraq and Egypt.

India was committed to organise this link within Iraq and to find the necessary staff and units. Out of the blue in July 1940 came a warning order putting me on ten days notice for this force as an Officer in the 'Field Security Police': this floored me as I had not heard of the FSP, nor had I any knowledge of their duties. I found out later that they had been formed originally in World War I to act as a kind of 'Special Branch' of The Military Police. Four newly raised sections had been in France in 1939–40, but after Dunkirk they had been transferred to the Intelligence Corps and renamed the Field Security Service.

I was expected to leave any at moment so my CO, very properly, deprived me of my Adjutancy. However, the two months of August and September went by without any further orders, but in October I was taken off ten days notice and put on indefinite notice. This made no difference to my position in the Battalion, and I became bored stiff with being merely an odd job man, doing Courts of Enquiry, without any real responsibilities. Luckily for me the Battalion's turn came to man Charbagh Fort; a two company 'Beau Geste' type post on the hills overlooking the Afghan frontier post of Torkham. The CO agreed that I should go there as permanent Commandant during our tour of duty. Here I experienced Intelligence in its lowest form; two men of the Battalion Intelligence Section, stationed in the Fort, made a daily observation through field glasses of the Afghan Post and compiled a Log, which no doubt finally found its way into the archives of the MI Directorate at Army HQ, Nothing of great moment was recorded and entries such as '3 Afghan soldiers came out' or '3 Afghan soldiers went in' were typical.

An amusing incident occurred while I was at Charbagh. It had been the custom to allow wives and lady friends of Officers stationed in Landi Kotal to travel up the Khyber Pass on Sundays to lunch at Landi Kotal. However to prevent annoyance to the Afghan Frontier Guards no one was allowed to go to the actual frontier, and in order to enforce this there was a road barrier a few miles out of Landi Kotal, but Officers stationed at Charbagh were granted passes to enable them to get to the Fort, and to carry out their duties. One Sunday, John Hudson, an Officer of my Regiment, invited the General's two charming daughters to come up from Peshawar and lunch in the 9th Gurkhas Mess, and as I knew them well from hunting with the Peshawar Vale Hounds, suggested that I joined them. During lunch John suggested that as I had a Torkham pass, I should take them down to see the frontier post. This I did, and duly delivered them back to Landi Kotal, from whence John drove them home. A day or so later I was sent for by the Brigade Major who asked me what I had done to upset the General. It transpired that a few days earlier an order had gone out stopping all visits to the Khyber by civilians, but for some reason the order had not reached Landi Kotal, so that when the General asked his daughters what they had done on Sunday and they replied 'Captain Hudson asked us to lunch at Landi Kotal, and Captain Mains took us down to Torkham', he blew his top and furious phone calls were made to discover why his orders had not been obeyed. The non receipt of the order put John Hudson in the clear, but not me, as I had no authority to take anyone down to Torkham. Luckily in the inquest that followed over the order going astray, my misdemeanour was overlooked.

Things finally got under way about the New Year 1941, when on a visit to the Peshawar Horse Show, I was told by a Staff Officer of District HQ that he believed that I had received a posting, but he did not know as to what or to where. On the same day, I met a friend, Captain 'Shackles' Majumdar of the 16th Light Cavalry, recently returned from a secondment to the RAF as an AILO; he said that he, also, had received a posting but had not yet seen it.

On my return to Landi Kotal I found a signal from Army HQ which read 'WARNING ORDER. Captain A. A. Mains appointed Instructor Class C at Intelligence School being formed at Bombay. Instruct Officer to report forthwith'. This ambiguous wording caused some head shaking, but District HQ ruled that 'Warning Order' should be disregarded in view of the 'report forthwith' so off I went to Bombay, 48 hours away by the Frontier Mail.

The Station Staff Officer, Bombay, to whom I reported, had no knowledge of the Intelligence School, except that there had been a proposal to locate it there, but that had come to nothing. I put up very comfortably at the Taj Mahal Hotel while the authorities sorted matters out. The errant School was located finally at Karachi so off I went again on a two night's train journey with two changes at Ahmadabad and Hyderabad (Sind). These journeys brought me into conflict with Military Accounts, who ruled that I should not have moved on a 'Warning Order' and, therefore should only be paid for the direct journey Peshawar to Karachi. The order from Peshawar District for me to move forthwith luckily overruled them. I had a further brush with the Accounts Department regarding my rate of pay while at the School. I was a substantive Lieutenant eligible for the higher rate of Lieutenant's pay, commonly known as the 'drunkards bob' (shilling), but I was also a war time temporary Captain, being paid as such. They raked up a ruling that I could either be a Captain, without the Instructor Class C's allowance or a Lieutenant with the allowance. As I would be on the higher rate of Lieutenant's pay the latter would be more advantageous financially, but would mean instructing, as a Lieutenant, acting or temporary Captains with possibly less service than I had. This, I decided, with reluctance, I could not do.

The Intelligence School was to be located in Old Government House, an attractive building in the best part of the town and standing in its own grounds. There I met the Commandant, Major 'Jock' Campbell, Royal Indian Army Service Corps; almost the first thing he said to me was 'do you know the third Instructor, a cavalry man called Majumdar'. This delighted me and the next morning I was standing on the platform, as the Mail from Lahore steamed in; Shackles face was a study when he saw me.

The setting up of the School was one of the many ill thought out and sometimes half baked schemes with which I had to deal during my time in Intelligence. Our resources in personnel and equipment were almost nil; we had a Commandant, Jock, a slow, soft speaking Scot, who used to tell everyone 'my name is Camp----Bell', a dear person, but no ball of fire and apt to get rattled when things were not going well. He was a very clever fellow, an interpreter in Persian and, I believe, in Pushto and Urdu also, and had been a Vice Consul in Iran before being recalled to military service. Shackles was the best of our bunch, an efficient likeable cavalry officer, who had done an Intelligence Course and better still had been an AILO; he was also a private pilot with considerable experience, so he was able to teach all aspects of RAF co-operation and Air Photo Interpretation from a practical angle. I was the juniormost Instructor, with no practical experience at all. We had been allotted two British clerks, but no Adjutant, Quartermaster or other administrative personnel. We had an empty building, no furniture, no specialised equipment and no stationery. We were spared, however, the trouble of looking after the students, anyway for the time being, as authority ruled that they should be billeted in a nearby Hotel. As I was the junior Instructor, I had also to take on the duties of Adjutant and Quartermaster; a very onerous task as we had only some ten days to get ready to receive the students as well as prepare our subjects.

The local military HQ had been ordered to assist us in every way possible, and we were lucky in that the General, Godfrey Hind, knew me as he was commanding the 2/2nd Gurkhas in Dehra Dun, when I joined the 2/9th. The GSO III(I) was

Captain Lewis Pugh, who had been an MIO in Calcutta, and later was the inspiration behind, as well as the Commander of, the 'unofficial' raid on Axis shipping in Goa harbour: he went out of his way to help us. Furniture for Lecture Halls and Offices was quickly forthcoming, but the snag was Typewriters, Duplicators and Stationery. Some of this could be indented for, but could not be issued in time and some was not military supply, so I was forced to pledge the Government's credit in the bazaar with such firms as Gestetners to obtain the Duplicators and the stationery to go with them.

Our brief was to teach Officers to hold the positions of Brigade and Battalion Intelligence Officers, with an inkling of the duties of a GSO III(I) of a Division. Jock took the general side of Intelligence, Shackles the RAF Liaison and Photo Interpretation, and it fell to me to deal with the rest — the running of Brigade and Battalion Intelligence Sections, situation maps and reports, road reconnaissances and so on.

The first course got under way without any great mishap, and half way through it Jock moved out of the Hotel into a Flat; this prompted Shackles and I to try the same thing, and the Station Staff Officer allotted us a very nice two bedroomed flat on the outskirts of the Cantonement on the road to the sea side suburb of Clifton. We also acquired secondhand a supercharged Mercedes sports car of somewhat antique vintage, which had been owned previously by some Maharaja. This had two disadvantages — the first was that the front floor boards were loose, so if you were showing off the cars' turn of speed to a girl while taking her home from a Club dance, they were apt to dislodge and send a gale up her skirts. The other was a defective spline in the gear box which could jam and the car was then immoveable. This happened for the first time outside the cinema. We had backed out across the main road and on attempting to go forward, nothing happened: the gear lever would not move nor would the car, in spite of enlisting a gang of helpers to push. An officious Constable told us to get it out of the way, and refused to believe us when we told him it was stuck. He called up another lot of pushers, so we wished him the best of luck, jumped into a taxi and went home. We were half way through dinner when we heard the unmistakeable sound of the 'Merc'. It had been brought back by a taxi driver, who explained that he knew the car, and all one had to do was to uncover the gear box and push the spline back by hand: he was duly rewarded.

Shackles had made contact with the RAF at Drigh Road airfield to find out if they could give the students short flights to teach them to observe and describe topographical features from low flying aircraft, but they could not take it on. A case was put up to hire aircraft from the Flying Club using Shackles whose 'ticket' allowed him to fly passengers as the pilot. Somewhat to our surprise this was agreed, and I decided to take advantage of this arrangement to get the Flying Club to study for my Pilot's licence. I never got it as I was posted away too soon but at least I had gone 'solo'.

Army HQ decided to save money by accommodating the students attending the second course on the first floor of Old Government House instead of in the Hotel, although they would continue to feed there. Once again the administrative arrangements fell to me; a very troublesome and time wasting business. Nearly a whole day was wasted in trying to get the Municipal water supply to fill the roof tanks. It never would have done had not someone discovered an underground tank in the garden into which this supply flowed and an electric pump to send it up to the roof.

We were about half way through the second course, when we were told to start planning for an Indian Wing, which would train Viceroys Commissioned Officers and Indian NCOs in unit Intelligence and Security duties. We selected two Officer Instructors designate. Captains Joe Hudson of the Baluch Regiment and Mani Ram Yadav of the Rajputana Rifles. Joe was an Interpreter in Arabic, so perhaps we were foolish in thinking that Army HQ would let us have him. In fact neither of these two Officers ever joined the Indian Wing. I also persuaded Jock Campbell to ask for a Subedar of my own battalion as Subedar Major. This Officer, Subedar Gajendra Malla, was a Gurkha from Dehra Dun District in India, and was extremely well educated and spoke excellent English. He had been the Battalion Intelligence Officer, and had run local courses for Battalion Intelligence sections, as well as instructing on a course for the Officers of two Nepalese Regiments. He had hardly taken up his appointment when he was commissioned and joined the Officer Instructors. He finished up at the end of the war as GSO III(I), before going even higher and achieving the rank of Colonel. It was a great disappointment to me that I never met him at the School as I had left before he arrived.

I was enjoying my time at the School; I liked instructing and Karachi was a far more civilised place than any I had previously been stationed in. I was very interested in my flying lessons and there was sailing, and bathing in the sea at Clifton. The war news was better than it had been for some time as Wavell had won a resounding victory over the Italians in the Western Desert, but a small cloud had appeared; this was the menacing pro Axis attitude of the Prime Minister of Iraq, Raschid Ali, who had ousted the boy King and his pro British Regent, Nuri Pasha as Said. The British battalion at Karachi had been flown off to reinforce the RAF station at Habbaniya in Iraq.

At the end of the second course, I went off on a few days leave to Lahore. The situation in Iraq had deteriorated, but as I was not with a unit, I presumed that it would have nothing to do with me. How wrong I was; on the second day of my leave I received a telegram of immediate recall. On my return, I found a posting order as a GSO III(I) overseas and instructions to report forthwith at Bombay for embarkation. Joe Hudson was posted also as a GSO III (Interpreter). I packed up my heavy kit and sent it off to the Regimental Centre with my servant, and I saw neither again for some four years, said my farewells, and set off for Bombay by the same route as that by which I had come.

CHAPTER TWO

Iraq 1941

O N arrival at Bombay, I learnt that I was to go to Iraq on the Troopship 'Nevasa', one of Transports which, in peace time, plied regularly between England and India and, curiously, the one in which I had originally come to India in 1934. The fact that I was a GSO III and that I was going to Iraq was about all I learnt, no mention of which HQ I would be a Staff Officer. There was nothing to grumble about at the moment; I was a graded Staff officer at the age of 27 and with only seven years service, something that I had never expected to happen. As India paid Staff Officers by grade and not by rank, I found my monthly pay had soared up to just short of one thousand Rupees, almost double that of a Captain.

The voyage was more like a pleasure cruise than an operation of war. Troopships had not yet gone 'dry' and the British India Line who managed the Nevasa had a reputation for good food. No sort of military activity was possible as no one knew what his job would be at the other end — I presumed that mine would be as a GSO III(I) of a Division. We arrived without incident off the mouth of the Shatt al Arab, and there anchored, as it was uncertain what sort of reception we should receive from the Iraqis; actually overt hostilities did not break out until the day after our arrival at Basra. The next day the Navy produced an escort for our convoy of three ships, and its size and composition showed to what straits the Royal Navy had been reduced in those waters; one small RN sloop, a smaller RIN sloop, and a RN 'China' gunboat. We passed up the Shatt without incident and in the evening docked at Margil, the port of Basra.

Basra by this time had become three separate towns, Basra City, Ashar and Maqu'il or Margil, as it was pronounced by foreigners, Basra City, the old port associated with Sinbad and the Arabian Nights was now several miles from the Shatt al Arab, and had ceased to be a Port. It had been replaced by Ashar on the river and this is where British and Indian forces were landed during World War I. It had no jetties, so ships had to lie offshore and unload into lighters. The Iraq Railways had built, in the inter war years, a new Port with rail served jetties at Margil, some two miles upstream from Ashar. The railway station was here also, and later, the international airport, with moorings nearby for the Imperial Airways flying boat service. A modern hotel had been built between the airport and the river, which was an overnight stop for both the flying boats and the KLM land aircraft.

Margil was laid out like a cross between an Indian Cantonement and an Indian Railway Town; straight streets crossing each other at right angles, with bungalows for the Port and Railway Officers set in large compounds with, of course, the inevitable Club. An imposing building near the dock gates housed the Head Quarters of the Iraq Ports and Railways Administration; equally imposing was the Director General, Colonel, or as he liked to be called, General Sir John Ward RE. He was an 'al Feriq' in the Iraq Army which was equivalent to a Lieutenant General. It was he who had supervised the building of Margil Port and brought it and the Railways to a high state of efficiency.

The Iraq Army had about a Brigade in or near the Basra area, but we found their conscripts somewhat lacking in fighting spirit; indeed far more dangerous were the armed sections of the Iraq Police. An ultimatum to the Iraq Government to cease the blockade of Habbaniya expired at mid day on the day after our arrival, so measures had to be taken for our defence. The two convoys that had already arrived had produced about a Brigade of fighting troops. There were also the indigenous Iraq Levies, raised to guard RAF airfields and installations, when

British ground forces had been withdrawn in the twenties. They were organised like the Indian Army; the Company Officers were British Officers seconded, but the platoons were commanded by Native Officers akin to Viceroys Commissioned Officers. They remained entirely loyal to the British cause, probably because they were recruited from Christian Assyrians, Kurds, and Shia Marsh Arabs, all at loggerheads with the ruling Sunni Arabs. These forces allowed us to man a tight perimeter at Margil taking in the airport and hotel, the RAF supply base on the river and the Makina Hospital a short distance inland.

I found out before long that the convoy in which I had arrived had contained the nucleus of three separate Headquarters — HQ Iraq Force, General Quinan, HQ Iraq L of C, General Beresford, and HQ 10th Indian Division, General Fraser. There was great confusion as to who was who, and this was not helped by the fact that the Brigade that had arrived and its supporting units had belonged to 9th Division. This Division was the one in the highest state of readiness and was earmarked for Malaya, and the Divisional Commander and some of his staff had already gone there to prepare for the arrival of his Division. Now as a matter of urgency these troops had to be switched to Iraq, with a new Commander and a Headquarters hastily flung together and renamed 10th Division. To add to the confusion some units were still using their old title such as 9th Divisional Signals. Matters were not improved by the Commander, General Fraser, having a nervous breakdown and being invalided. This, however proved a blessing in disguise as the Force Commander selected his Brigadier General Staff as the replacement, and thus gave Bill Slim his first Divisional command.

The ships of the two convoys had been sent off in great haste and had not been tactically loaded; indeed they had been loaded on no plan at all. Units had arrived at Bombay partially mobilised and much of their mobilisation equipment had been sent from the Ordnance depots direct to the docks. The whole lot was literally poured into the ships hugger-mugger, and thus it came out onto the jetties at Margil, in the same state, causing considerable congestion while it was being sorted out. The same applied to the various Headquarters; instead of the Commander and his Staff travelling together as an entity, the various Staff Officers, like myself, were ordered to Bombay and put on the first available ship.

Joe Hudson and I were sent on arrival to join 10th Division HQ; a very makeshift affair with Officers pulled in from anywhere. The Intelligence Staff consisted of two RAF Officers, Squadron Leaders Coates and Embling, the Special Service Officers Bahrain and Basra respectively. Joe, as an Arabic speaker, met with some favour in their eyes but I none, and as a result, was given the menial task of enciphering and deciphering long telegrams to and from the Air Ministry. These Special Service Officers were more akin to Political than Intelligence Officers having considerable independence and dealing direct with the Air Ministry. Their local knowledge was a great help to the Force Commander, but on several occasions they tried to dictate to him. Once they told him that he must occupy Basra City immediately, as they believed that the Iraq Army was about to burn down the Land Registry building, housing the records of the date plantations in Iraq of the Sheikh of Kuwait, an ally of Britain; on another occasion they woke up General Quinan in the middle of the night, with a story that Raschid Ali was about to murder the boy King and his uncle the Regent. The General was not amused as there were no British troops anywhere near Bagdad, and even if the story was true there was nothing he could do about it.

After a while I got bored with my job in ciphers and approached the acting GSO I, Colonel (later General) Ouvry Roberts, saying that this did not seem to be the work for which I had been either trained or selected; all I got was a bawling out and an order to get back and do as I was told. However, relief was at hand, as, although I did not know it, it transpired that I was the GSO III(I) of Force HQ, and the only Intelligence Staff Officer to have arrived to date, General Quinan and his BGS, Bill Slim, had been trying to discover my whereabouts, so in due course, I was discovered in 10th Div HQ, and received — a peremptory order to report to Force HQ at the Margil Club. The first task that I was given, illustrated vividly the confusion that existed, because it was to ascertain what

British units had arrived and where they were located; Intelligence about the enemy was of secondary importance.

The arrangements for our accommodation and feeding were equally chaotic. Officers from the Nevasa had spent the first night ashore in the Officer's quarters of the Makina Hospital, but we were kicked out of there to make room for a party of Nursing Sisters, who had originally been accommodated at the Airport Hotel, but which now was considered too close to our perimeter for safety. About a dozen of us were sent to a semi derelict river steamer moored off the RAF enclave. This was not too uncomfortable, as the senior, I took the Captain's single berth cabin, the remainder were in double cabins, except for one officer who annexed the semi enclosed bridge.

The next problem was how and by whom were we to be fed. The Indian Army was endeavouring to abolish the private personal and mess servants which had been common on active service in World War I, and to replace them by 'Mess Units'. These comprised a Butler, Cook and Waiters, together with Water Carriers, Sweepers and other menials. We acquired one of these, probably one of the first to be used, but this did not immediately solve our problem. The Cook could cook, the Butlers and Waiters could wait, but no one had instructed them as to how or where they could draw rations or buy fresh produce, and the RAF's NAAFI was unhelpful, at first refusing service on the grounds that we did not belong to the RAF, nor even to the British Army. However, with some waste of time, we overcame our difficulties and made ourselves reasonably comfortable. This, of course, was the signal to higher authority to move us again, this time to the Old Quarantine Camp. This place may have been luxurious for pilgrims but was distinctly uncomfortable for us. We were rescued from here by the GOC Lines of Communications, General 'Squeaky George' Beresford, who was horrified at the conditions under which we were living. Our next move was to real luxury, air conditioned bedrooms in the Airport Hotel; our mess unit set up shop on the lawn outside the rear entrance, and we had the Air Passengers Waiting room as our Mess.

FIELD SECURITY

The military position at Basra was frustrating as by now we had a good build up of troops and should have been able to advance on Bagdad without any great difficulty, had it not been for exceptionally severe floods which prevented any forward movement. Bagdad was captured and the King restored not by us, but by a mixed force of Household Cavalry and Arab Legion, in soft trucks, who came across the Desert from Palestine. Meanwhile the steady build up of Axis air strength in Syria with the co-operation of the Vichy High Commissioner, General Dentz, necessitated an advance from Palestine to oust the Vichy regime and replace it by the Free French. Iraq Force played a part in this, as immediately the floods subsided, Bill Slim led out 10th Division, by-passing Bagdad, into Eastern Syria. This was a great feat as the Division had never before acted as an entity, and the MT move of over 600 miles was accomplished by Indian drivers who six months before had never driven a vehicle. He arrived at Deir es Zor defeated a force of the Foreign Legion and secured that part of Syria.

While all this was going on, the Intelligence set up of Iraq Force was taking shape; two Staff Officers senior to me arrived, Lieutenant Colonel Tony Boyce as GSO I and Head of the Intelligence Section and a Major Fitzpatrick as GSO II. Tony Boyce, of the 14th Punjab Regiment, was an experienced Intelligence Officer, a most delightful person to work for, with an impressive war record in World War I when he had won both the Military Cross and the Military Medal. 'Fitz' was a British Service Officer, who had just passed out from the Staff College at Quetta, but had no experience in Intelligence. Tony Boyce decided to give the Operational Intelligence sub section (Ia) to 'Fitz' and the Security sub section (Ib) to me as he thought that I was more suited to this work by virtue of having done a Command Intelligence Course; and this is how I was launched into Security.

Two Intelligence units arrived from Karachi at this time, Nos. 1 & 2 L of C Intelligence Sections, each comprising a Commandant, for administration only, a Censorship Section, and part of a Field Security Section. The part FS Section consisted of a Field Security Officer, a Jemadar and six Indian ranks, and some transport; British ranks and motor cycles were to be supplied by the British Government in due course. The two Field Security Officers were Captain Mani Ram Yadav of the Rajputana Rifles and Lieutenant Evans of the Worcestershire Regiment, both students on our first Karachi course and destined to be the first two FSOs of the Indian Intelligence Corps. We were hoping that we might get the missing British ranks of the FS Sections from HQ Middle East so that these sections could work as complete entities. The L of C Intelligence Sections seemed unlikely ever to work as separate units so they were disbanded: the FS part in due course became part of our new Iraq Composite FS Sections, the Censors set up on their own, under the Force Chief Censor, and the Commandants were reposted to other jobs.

Nothing very much had been achieved, by the time Force HQ moved to Bagdad, where we took over a number of reasonably modern European houses on the west bank of the Tigris between the railway station and the river. Intelligence was allotted a large two storied house on the river embankment.

There were difficulties on the political and diplomatic front. The restored Government, under the new Prime Minister, Jamil Mad'fai, broke off diplomatic relations with the Axis, but did not declare war; this led to the awkward position of a British occupying force in a neutral country and gave us some security problems, as we could not infringe Iraq's sovereignty in her own country. There was still a certain amount of anti British feeling both in the country and Iraq Government agencies, particularly in the Police, and the Government, itself, was too weak to do much about it. Cases occurred of British Officers being spat at in the streets and deliberate attempts were made to run them over when crossing the road. Our Ambassador protested strongly, causing the Premier to be dismissed and replaced by that good friend of Britain, Nuri Pasha. He issued orders to the Bagdad Police that any such behaviour was to be dealt with by a summary beating on the spot.

Shortly after our arrival in Bagdad, Nos. 71 and 72 British Field Security Sections, under the command of Captains Martin and Scott, arrived from the Middle East Depot. These sections were typical of the earlier British sections; all the Other Ranks being men of good education, and nearly all speaking one, if not more, European languages. We now had two good British sections each consisting of a Sergeant Major and twelve British Other Ranks, with twelve motor cycles, two untrained Indian sections of a Viceroys Commissioned Officer and twelve Indian ranks, with one or two 15 cwt trucks, together with four Field Security Officers, two experienced and two, Yadav and Evans, with, as yet, little experience. I suggested to Tony Boyce that rear units such as Headquarters, Depots, transportation and supply troops were much more vulnerable than fighting formations, so we should concentrate on covering them and leave 10th Indian Division for the time being. The division of our sections into halves and the linking of a British and an Indian half to form one composite section gave us the first four Field Security Sections of the Indian Intelligence Corps, although they were not to be so called until late 1942; for the time being they would be named Nos. 1, 2, 3 and 4 Iraq Composite Field Security Sections.

Martin and Scott, of course, would command two of the sections and I was confident that Evans would make good with the third, but I was not so certain about Yadav. Mani Ram was a good officer and comrade, but, although he was a graduate of the Indian Military Academy, I considered that he had neither the temperament nor tact for an L of C section nor to command British soldiers. I would hasten to say that this was not general, a Gurkha VCO of my Regiment was commissioned at Karachi, without any officer training, and commanded a composite section of 4th Indian Division in Greece with considerable distinction. Mani Ram was a good trainer of Indian soldiers, so it was decided to send him to raise and train an all Indian section for 10th Division. One of the Sergeant Majors, Henderson, who had come from the Middle East, had an impressive peace time record, both in the Hotel and the Tourist trade. He had done his training in the LMS Hotels and at the Negresco in Nice, and at the time of his enlistment was employed by Lunn's Tours, so he was commissioned to command the fourth section. The final set up was No. 1 Section, Henderson, at Basra; No. 2 Martin, Shaiba Base; No. 3 Scott, Railway section based on Bagdad, and No. 4, Evans at Bagdad.

We had hardly got this organised when trouble arose in Iran necessitating the capture of the Abadan Refinery and the southern part of the pipeline by the 18th Indian Brigade of the newly arrived 8th Indian Division. 10th Division also crossed into Iran further north and captured Kermanshah. The Shah then abdicated in favour of his son, who agreed to the occupation of the southern half of the country by British Forces and the northern by the Russians. The north-south railway became one of the supply routes to Russia. This had little effect on us at the time, except that arrangements had to be made for Divisional sections both for the 8th Division and for the 6th Indian Division, which arrived later. There was no doubt that when the L of C to Russia really got under way, which was not until the following year, security cover would be required. I was intending to carry out a reconnaissance in January 1942, but I was posted to Burma before I was able to do it.

Our work could be divided into routine unit security and the more glamourous counter espionage. We had to start from scratch with the former as all our units had been in peace time conditions before leaving India, and a great deal of security education was necessary. We were constantly coming up against senior officers who resented us and our brief. One argument often used was that the time taken to check identity documents and passes at Depots and similar installations would slow up movement to an unacceptable degree. A British NCO on a night security patrol managed to penetrate into the unlocked office of the Director of Transportation and removed a secret document lying on his desk; the offender, a peppery Colonel, tried to run me in before the Force Commander for every crime in the Calendar, but Tony Boyce was able to smoothe matters over.

We were much hampered by the fact that two years after the outbreak of war, India had not yet introduced Officer's Identity Cards. We got over this by getting both the Identity Cards and the Record Cards printed by the Middle East Security Press and paid for out of the Secret Intelligence Grant, usually known as the 'Slush Fund'. The issue of the Cards was a major achievement as the Force now comprised three Divisions, as well as Base and L of C units. The Record cards were indexed and kept in the I(b) office, and this was a full time job for one Intelligence Officer.

The Counter espionage part of our work was much more interesting. The final section of the original 'Berlin — Bagdad Bahn' had been completed in 1940, and the 'Taurus Express', including a through Sleeping Car and Restaurant Car of the Wagon Lits Company was running twice a week between Hyder Pasha (Istanbul) and Bagdad. This was one of the only two ways from Axis territory to the rest of the world; the other was via Spain and Portugal. Iraq's neutrality made this an acceptable route for enemy agents as well as for bona fide travellers, and so it was desirable that some control be exercised, not only to deter such agents, but, also, to glean information from those who had been residing in Germany.

We had to overcome some diplomatic objections; the major being that we could not carry out any passport or customs control on Iraq territory, but we were lucky that the railway had to cross a strip of about 60 miles of Syria between Iraq and Turkey,and this country was now governed by our allies, the Free French. We were fortunate, also, that the control station, Tel Kotchek, on the Iraq-Syrian frontier was physically on Syrian soil so we could set up there what controls we liked. We needed the co-operation of the Wagon Lit staff, particularly the Sleeping Car conductors. These men were employed by the Turkish Division of the Wagon Lit Company, and, as Paris, the Headquarters of the Company was in German hands, it was effectively controlled by them. The local agents in Bagdad, who did the bookings and provisioned the Restaurant car, were Thomas Cook & Co Ltd, a British Company, which, as it had become a subsidary of the WL, was managed by the Controller of Enemy Property in London. The Turkish employees travelled on special Identity cards issued by the Company in Ankara, which were recognised by the Turkish, Syrian and Iraqi authorities. I had noticed during pre war journeys in Europe, that passengers in WL Sleeping Cars were rarely disturbed at night for Passport or Customs controls.

The reason, I presumed, was that the Car Conductors were required to provide information about passengers to the Police and other agencies at the various frontiers. I decided, therefore, that they should do for us what they were undoubtedly doing for the Police of their own country, as well as for the Syrian Sureté.

Before I could start on this or any other methods of control, I had to find suitable personnel; luckily these were available from among the British FS NCOs who had come from the Middle East. I selected about four, who had good language qualifications, withdrew them from their sections, attached them for administration to No. 3 (Railway) Section, and sent them off to Tel Kotchek, naming them the Iraq FS Special Branch. They came under the direct command of I(b) Branch and their duties were two fold — first, they were to assist the Syrian Sureté and Customs in their control of passengers and the searching of baggage and the train generally; although they were to interest themselves only in the intelligence aspect and not in smuggling or anything of that kind. They were to list all through passengers, with nationality, passport numbers and reasons for travel. This list was sent to us, where it was copied for a number of intelligence agencies; I cannot remember them all, but it certainly went to the Intelligence Branches of HQs Middle East and 9th Army, Security Intelligence Middle East (SIME), the British Embassy Bagdad, and, I think to London also. To facilitate the passage of our controls, VIPs, allied or neutral, recommended by the British Embassy were issued with a 'laisser passer' and their passports stamped by us to record the fact.

The Special Branch's second task was the gaining of information from travellers, who had come from Germany or other Axis countries. The control NCO at Tel Kotchek would ascertain if there were any such on the train, and, if so, warn his colleague on the train, who would contact the persons concerned, usually over a drink in the Restaurant car, and if there was any interesting information to be gained, an Intelligence Officer would call on the traveller at his Bagdad Hotel. A group of Chinese students gave much valuable information about conditions in Berlin and the effect of the allied bombing.

We got full co-operation from the Syrian authorities at Tel Kotchek, but not at first from the Turkish WL employees. To 'encourage their co-operation', I started to make a nuisance of myself by instructing my FS NCOs to carry out exceptionally rigorous searches of the Sleeping and Restaurant cars while they were on Syrian territory. This included pulling the bedding off the sleeping car berths and ransacking the linen cupboards, and in the restaurant car, taking the food out of the ice box, unscrewing the advertisements, searching the various cupboards and leaving the staff to put it all back again. One might ask what effect this had on the running of the train — the short answer was that it made it very late, but this was a minor matter, and anyway, the southbound train normally arrived on our territory some eight to twelve hours late by the time the Turks and Syrians had done their searches each side of Aleppo; our ministrations only made it later. The Turkish staff soon discovered that it paid to co-operate, particularly as we paid for information. Most of them became my good friends and I was assured of first class service everytime I travelled.

I hope that our statistical information was of interest to the more sophisticated Intelligence organisations, and we certainly had one interesting catch, a Vichy French Officer. He turned up in Bagdad, having come in from Turkey direct by mule trail, and requested our Embassy to issue him with a 'laisser passer' to proceed to Kabul via India where he had been appointed Military Attaché. He stayed in a Hotel in Bagdad, while his case was being considered, and where he was visited by our Intelligence Officers; I took him to dinner one day. He spoke excellent English and professed pro British sentiments. He was also an expert in Camel Corps tactics and had written a book on this subject entitled 'Le Mehariste'. Ultimately his request was refused and he decided to return to Turkey by train. He must have been either incredibly stupid in thinking that we would allow him to go free on Allied soil ie Syria or, more likely, he thought that as a French Officer he could browbeat the Syrian officals. He miscalculated as regards the latter as he would have to pass my Special Branch control, and while the Chef de Sureté at Tel Kotchek was a Syrian, the Chef de Douane was a pro British Frenchman.

The upshot was that he was hauled off the train and he and his luggage thoroughly searched when some incriminating items were found, so he was duly arrested. The matter was then referred to HQ 9th Army as Tel Kotchek was in their jurisdiction, although for convenience we were doing the Security work right up to the Turkish frontier. The case was referred again to General Catroux, de Gaulle's Delegué General in Syria, who promptly released him.

All these commitments meant that the I(b) section had expanded considerably, and now had four Intelligence Officers as well as myself as section head. The one room that we had been occupying in the 'Intelligence' house was now too cramped so we moved into premises of our own, a bungalow a short distance from the main office. Our standing now merited a GSO II as section head and the BGS accepted Tony Boyce's recommendation that I should be upgraded into that appointment. It was unfortunate that this had to be sanctioned by Army HQ, India, who flatly refused to upgrade me on the grounds of my age and length of service. They argued that most existing GSO IIIs were considerably senior to me, and officers coming off Staff College courses, some three or four years my senior, were only receiving third grade appointments. This was rather ridiculous as British Army officers were serving in England and the Middle East as GSO IIs if they had the necessary knowledge and experience, and, anyway, India was going to appoint me as one in another five months or so.

The BGS very kindly offered to get me a vacancy on the next Staff College course, proceeded by a months leave. This was a tempting offer but I declined it, I felt that as I was the pioneer of Security Intelligence in the Indian Army, I would like to continue in it, and certainly in Iraq where much remained to be done. The problem was, if I remained, who was to supersede me as there was no one in Iraq who had any specialised knowledge of Security. The BGS came up finally with a cunning, but wholly acceptable, solution. There was a GSO III serving in the Operations branch, who was considerably senior to me and due for upgrading. He was none other than my friend, John Hudson, of my own battalion, who had brought down the General's wrath upon me when he had escorted the latter's daughters to lunch in Landi Kotal the year before. He had the reputation of standing up for his subordinates, even when they were in the wrong, and of delegating work as much as possible. Although he had no knowledge of Security work the BGS considered that we would make a good team, with me doing the work and John fending off the fast balls.

I was still entitled to a months leave out of Iraq, but I considered that I could have a break and at the same time learn my trade with the British Field Security sections in Syria and the Lebanon, and, also, if I visited HQ 9th Army, I could regularise the position of the 'Duck's Bill', the 60 mile strip of Syrian territory across which the railway ran between Iraq and Turkey. Tony Boyce accepted my proposal that I should have an official 'tour' to HQ 9th Army. This meant that I should have my fares paid, but as I was going for a month, I agreed to pay my Hotel bills and work on liason duties for 50% of the time. He agreed, also, that I should travel by rail to Aleppo through Turkey.

The Treaty of Sevres in 1922, which ended the War with Turkey, had drawn the Frontier irrespective of the line of the railway, the Berlin — Bagdad Bahn. It now entered Syria in the Kurd Dagh Mountains, north west of Aleppo, reversed at Aleppo, and then ran north east to re-enter Turkey; and from then on to the frontier station of Nusaybin, where it again entered Syria at the 'Ducks' Bill', it ran literally along the frontier, but just within Turkey. The French and the Turks had an agreement by which military personnel of either could travel from one part of their territory to the other in uniform, and without formalities. This still applied to the Free French, but not to the British forces, so to avoid internment, I had to travel as a civilian.

I had nearly been interned earlier when I was staying with Joe Hudson, who had become our Political Officer at Kamechlie. We had been invited to attend the celebrations of the Turkish National Day at Nusaybin, and when taking a new route over the frontier, we ran into a Turkish post, whose soldiers politely but firmly refused to let us go without permission from their HQ; as all the Officers were attending the celebrations, it was some time before a Captain arrived to rescue us. A diplomatic exchange then took place in French; he said that the soldiers had exceeded their authority and would be punished, and we countered that the soldiers had done their duty in an exemplary manner and should be rewarded. What was galling was that the Turkish post was only a hundred yards from a road along which our lorries were passing.

The first thing I did in preparing for my journey was to get the British Consul to issue me with a Passport in which I was described as a 'British Government Servant'; this entitled me also to a free Turkish visa, which the Consul obtained for me. I then bought some civilian clothes for the journey, and booked my sleeping car berth to Aleppo with Thomas Cook. The last item was to send one of our local interpreters to change Iraq Dinars into Syrian Pounds in the Souk, where there was a better rate of exchange than with the Field Cashier and thus technically forbidden.

The Taurus Express on which I travelled was a curious cross between a 'Train de Luxe' and a mixed Passenger and Goods. It had been running for some years, but only as far as Nusaybin, from where a road connection took through passengers to Kirkuk, the northern railhead of the Iraq metre gauge system. The standard gauge section only went as far as Samarra, sixty miles north of Bagdad, leaving a considerable gap. This section was very short of rolling stock and what it had was very primitive, unlike the metre gauge network which boasted restaurant cars and air conditioned sleepers. The link up with the Syrian and Turkish systems had taken place in 1940, and the Iraq railways now had a standard gauge section of nearly three hundred miles with little motive power or rolling stock. The position improved before I left Iraq as a number of passenger coaches en route from Germany to Iran were commandeered, later, in view of Iraq's increased strategic importance, some British locomotives were received.

The actual train, which left Bagdad twice a week consisted of three blue WL vehicles, a sleeping car, restaurant car and a fourgon or luggage van such as would have been found in European 'trains de luxe'; these were for Istanbul. The remainder of the train, one antique 1st and 2nd class carriage and a collection of four wheeled 3rd class, actually good vehicles converted to seating accommodation, only went as far as Mosul. The motive power was an original Berlin — Bagdad Bahn locomotive built by Borsig of Berlin about 1914.

On arrival at Mosul after the overnight run from Bagdad, the Iraq coaches were taken off and replaced by two European type Syrian coaches, one 1st and 2nd and one 3rd class, and behind them a long train of goods wagons. Thus we progressed to Tel Kotchek, where, while the passport and customs controls were under way, the train was again re-marshalled, some of the goods wagons being taken off and others put on. The locomotive was replaced by another identical one, but instead of 'I. R.', Iraq Railways, the new one had 'L. S. B.', Ligne Syrian à Bagdad. We now left behind the English type of operation, with fixed signals at every station, for a much more primitive system. In place of signals, a pointsman sitting on the point lever at the entrance of a station with red and green flags and lamps sufficed. On arrival at Nusaybin, we lost the goods wagons, and acquired an enormous modern German built Turkish locomotive, but on arrival at Aleppo on the second morning, we had reverted once more to a mixed train.

Once in Aleppo, I put up at the best Hotel, the Barron, and set about contacting the local British HQ and the Field Security Section. They were most helpful and allowed me to see all aspects of their Security work. I also did some sightseeing visiting the famous Citadel and the Souk, where, through the good offices of a Syrian Police Officer, le Commissaire Hadji Tooma, I purchased some dark brown real camel hair cloth, which I took to a tailor with the delightful name of 'Au Poilu de France' to be made into a quasi military type greatcoat. Regrettably, it was lost with the rest of my kit in the Burma Retreat.

I was able to take part in one very interesting operation; the spiriting away to a British Interrogation Centre, without the knowledge of his friends, of a suspect arriving by train from Turkey. I went with the FSO and two of his men by car to the Frontier Post in the Kurd Dagh mountains. While we were awaiting the arrival of the train, we were entertained by the Armenian Headman of the village, who was a great admirer of Churchill. The train, having arrived, we boarded it, together with the men of the Syrian Sureté, who went along the train collecting traveller's Passports and bringing them to the Restaurant Car for examination and the preparation of the entry lists. We were all drinking together, when the FSO managed to purloin the suspect's passport, without the men of the Surete noticing and, after his name had been recorded. The rest was easy, a station or so further on and the man was lured to the carriage door on the pretext that there was a message awaiting him, then a boot in his backside propelled him into the waiting arms of the FS, who put him into a vehicle and drove him away. The FSO and I then retired to an empty first class compartment and slept until we arrived back in Aleppo. When the suspect's friends found out that he was not on the train, they went to the Sureté, who could only tell them that he must have entered the country as his name was on the entry list for the train in question.

After a week in Aleppo, I set off for Beirut by train. The railway to the south was a French sponsored concern, the 'Chemin de fer de Damas, Hama et Prolongements', or 'DHP' for short; this ran due south through Hama and Homs to a junction with the narrow gauge Beirut to Damascus line in the Bekaa Valley near Baalbek. The quickest way to Beirut, was by the daily railcar which branched off the mainline at Homs and ran through the mountains to terminate by the sea at Tripoli, where it connected with a bus to Beirut. This was an interesting journey, passing the great waterwheels at Hama, and then the section through the mountains with the famous Crusader fortress, the 'Krak des Chevaliers' showing up on a mountain to the north. Within a year the Royal Engineers had constructed a link down the coast through Beirut to meet the Palestine Railways at Acre; sadly the southern portion fell into disuse on the establishment of the State of Israel, but the northern section continued for some time with a through railcar from Aleppo to Beirut, but the troubles in the Lebanon have caused this to be withdrawn also.

Having enlarged on the railway system to Beirut, I ought to try and explain the somewhat chaotic civil and military set up in the country. Syria, as a whole, was a League of Nations mandate granted to the French. It was classified as a territory, which should be ready for self rule in a relatively short time. Iraq was a similar mandate given to the British, who had already granted self government. The French, however, were determined to delay any hand over as long as possible, and to this end had organised the Government in such a way as to play off the various races and religions against each other.

The Mandate was split into four administrative regions; the Sunni Moslem 'Etat du Syrie', the Christian 'Etat du Grand Liban', I say Christian advisedly as there was a sizeable Moslem minority, Sunnis in the north and Shias in the south, together with the two 'Gouvernments' of Latakia and the Jebel Druse, the former having been previously known as the State of the Allaouites; the Allaouites and the Druse being two heretical Moslem sects. A certain measure of self government was allowed, particularly in the two 'Etats', with native officers in the administration and police, but the French kept a very tight control. The situation was not unlike that which pertained in the Indian Native States, where 'advice' given by the Government of India was 'paramount' and had to be obeyed. The French had gone further than this and French Officers, seconded from the Army, were to be found in all branches of the administration but specially in the Sureté General, the CID or Special Branch. Another facet of their rule was the posting to the remoter Districts of an 'Officer du Service Speciale' with his own military force, a Squadron of Christian Circassians, to oversee the native Magistrate and Chief of Police. The defeat of the Vichy forces had made little difference to the administration, merely the substitution of Free French for Vichy and General Catroux, de Gaulle's, Delegué General for General Dentz, Vichy's High Commissioner. The administration went on much as before, as, while most of the French Officers of the fighting forces opted for repatriation, most in the administration found their jobs too lucrative to give up for a principle. Few were pro de Gaulle, but many were actively pro Vichy, which did not aid Catroux in his task. The French soldiers, mostly Foreign Legion and Senegalese, for the most part followed their Officers and opted for repatriation; although I was told by some British Officers that the Legionaires were so drunk that they had to be hoisted onto the ships in nets.

The British military set up was nearly as complicated. HQ 9th Army situated in Broumana, in the mountains above Beirut, commanded all Allied Forces in the mandates of Palestine and Syria. The British Army provided the Intelligence, Supply and Transportation troops, but the fighting force was the 7th Australian Division. This formation was not in the highest state of either discipline or morale. They detested their static garrison role, the country and its people, and most of all the French; the latter was largely due to their defeat by the Foreign Legion and Senegalese during the advance into Syria. They had been led to believe that it would be a walk over and that they would be greeted as liberators, so it was a nasty shock when they came up against stiff resistance. There was an unpleasant incident in north Syria not long after my arrival in Beirut, when a party of Australians, all drunk, crashed a vehicle through a Turkish Post and the Turks opened fire and killed the lot.

Once in Beirut the Hotel Normandie became my very comfortable base, and, true to my bargain with Tony Boyce, I made contact with the British FSO in Beirut. He was most helpful and allowed me to accompany him on his various duties. I used to telephone him each morning to enquire if he had anything interesting on, and, if there was not, I would suggest that we met for lunch at the French Officers Club, the 'Cercle', where the best food in Beirut was to be had. I visited HQ 9th Army, and, also, HQ 7th Australian Division; discussions with the Intelligence Staff of the former led to a formal agreement that we, in Iraq, should deal with railway security and intelligence across the 'Duck's Bill' right up to the Turkish frontier. I was lucky in being able to get a day trip to Damascus, ostensibly to visit the FSO there, but actually to do some sight seeing.

While I was working with the Beirut FS Section, I was involved in an incident with Australian troops, which could have turned nasty. The FSO wanted to grab a local prostitute, who was suspected of being a Turkish agent, out of the brothel in which she worked, take her back to her flat and search it for incriminating material. The military and civil set up required the co-operation of various agencies, which necessitated a ridiculously large party; the FSO, myself and two of his men all in mufti, two British MPs in uniform, two 'agents' from the 'Police of Morals', who were responsible for good order in the red light district, and finally the 'Brigadier' (Police Sergeant) and two men from the local police station. This large party caused much alarm and despondency to Madame, the girls and the customers. At one period, while the girl was still being sought, the FSO and I were threatened by a party of Australians in a highly belligerent mood. When they advanced towards us, the British MPs having disappeared, I wondered whether I should draw my 9mm Walther Automatic from one pocket or my rubber cosh from the other. Luckily at that moment the rest of our party reappeared with the girl and we beat a hasty retreat. The search of the flat was a damp squib as far as Intelligence was concerned, but not for the MPs, as a large quantity of purloined British rations was discovered, together with the cap of a British Officer.

My month soon came to an end, and I was on my way back to Iraq by the same route as that by which I had come. I took the overnight train from Tripoli to Aleppo, spending a comfortable night in an old teak sided Wagon Lit of a type already obsolete in Europe, which creaked and groaned on its way at about 20 mph, arriving in Aleppo in time for breakfast.

The Taurus, as usual, was very late and by late afternoon of the next day we had still not reached Nusaybin, and were proceeding along the frontier but inside Turkey, when there was a crash and one of the windows in the corridor, on the Syrian side, was smashed to pieces, followed immediately by another. I deduced that someone must be shooting at us, so I went smartly to ground on the floor of my compartment. Nothing further happened and soon the 'Chef de Train' appeared with the sleeping car attendant and a Turkish policeman. They searched about in the broken glass and found two round stones. Shades of David and Goliath — the local Bedouin had used their slings to stone the train, just for fun. Later the Attendant came to me and said in French — 'Monsieur, I see from your Passport that you are Monsieur Mains, a British Government Servant, but I know that you are le Capitaine Mains, the Passport controller of the British Army in Iraq, Mon Capitaine, when we cross the border your Sergeant will come with the Syrian Sureté to check the Passports, ask him, on his return to Kamechlié, to see the French "Officier du Service Speciale" and get him to send out his Circassians to beat up those Bedouin'.

On return to duty, I found an unusual and potentially difficult task looming up. There were still a sizeable number of Axis nationals in Iran and Afghanistan, and the Governments concerned had been persuaded to break off diplomatic relations and expel them, but only on the condition that the British arranged their journey home under a safe conduct. It was obvious that the only feasible way for them to travel would be via Iraq and Istanbul, and thus a great deal of work was going to be thrown on to HQ Iraq Force.

The Afghanistan party would have to be brought down in buses and lorries through the Khyber pass to Peshawar, then by special train to Karachi, ship to Basra and onward by rail with a change of train and station at Bagdad. The Iran party was easier; road to Bagdad and onward direct by train. Difficulties arose from the beginning — the major one was the acute shortage of rolling stock in Iraq, both standard and metre gauge. Then there was the problem of using Iraqi stock on the

Bagdad to Istanbul run; how long would it be before the Iraq Railways got it back, if at all. The problem was made more acute by the edict that I or II class upholstered coaches must be provided, no III class hard wooden seats.

Our Transportation Branch solved the standard gauge problem, by hiring from the Turkish Railways two complete trains, each with a WL Restaurant Car, but the only way that stock could be provided for the metre gauge portion of the journey was to reduce the number of upper class carriages on the daily Mail train by about two thirds, causing great annoyance and grumbling. There was a reasonable amount of non corridor stock, but these were ruled out for security reasons, as the guards would not be able to patrol the moving train.

There was another aspect of the problem which was of vital interest to the Security Branch. A possible attack on the Allied oil supplies, either through Turkey or the Caucasus, had led to a steady build up of both troops and war like stores in Iraq. The paucity of roads had caused both Camps and Depots to be sited near to the railway at Basra, Bagdad and Mosul, and it seemed obvious to us that these Axis nationals should not be allowed to see them. Our solution was to have the disembarkation and entrainment at Basra during the hours of darkness. The train would lie up at a wayside station in the desert the next day, and come into Bagdad for the transhipment after dark. The same would apply on the next section, Mosul also being passed in the dark. Similar arrangements were proposed for the Iran party. All hell broke loose on us when our plan was proposed. It was unnecessary and impossible, it would tie up too much rolling stock, increase the hire charges of the Turkish trains, cause difficulties in feeding the party between Basra and Bagdad were only some of the objections. Finally Tony Boyce took the matter to the General, who came down on our side and all was well.

The next headache was security during the passage through Iraq. The Afghanistan party had an escort of British soldiers, who had come from India and were going through to the Turkish frontier; the escort for the Iran party would be provided from Iraq Force. The Indian escort was extremely lackadaisical, with no idea of security. They maintained that none of their party would try to escape as they were going home, and looked on the whole affair as a pleasure trip. To try and get our message across, I sent two German speaking NCOs from the Special Branch down to Basra to assist the Escort Commander, and went, myself, to join the train at a station outside Bagdad to explain the transhipment arrangements in detail.

The fact that Iraq was a neutral and independant State complicated these arrangements. The Iraq authorities insisted that they should police the Stations, but we did not want any of the Police to come in contact with the Axis party. By no means all the pro Raschid Ali and pro Axis Police Officers had been purged by the Nuri Government, and there was a possibility of undesirable contacts. A number of meetings were held under the auspices of the British Director General of the Iraq CID, and the final plan was that the Bagdad Town Police would find the outer cordon to keep away sightseers. The Military Police assisted by the Field Security would oversee the transhipment, and to get over Iraqi objections, one or two specially chosen CID officers would be allowed on the platforms. All went smoothly, except that the Brigadier commanding the Bagdad Sub Area mistook one of the CID men for an unauthorised civilian and ordered the nearest Military Policeman to arrest him, but luckily an FS NCO was able to explain matters before they got out of hand.

Shortly after these events, I paid another, and as it turned out, a final visit to Kamechlié. This was ostensibly to show John Hudson the arrangements at the frontier; 'to inspect the Passport Post at Tel Kotchek' was the official reason, but I had also heard that the Jezireh, the semi desert plateau in northern Iraq and extending into Syria, was world famous for sand grouse, John was a keen shikari, and I was sure that Joe Hudson could lay on a shoot for us, borrowing guns from the local officials. The shoot went off very well, the birds coming over in droves.

It was now December, and I was contemplating a visit to the other end of my 'manor', Iran, when I was sent for by Tony Boyce with two pieces of news. The first was that he had recommended me for an MBE, but regrettably the honour was down graded to a 'Mention in Dispatches', and, in fact, this was not gazzetted for nearly a year, unlike the 'Mention', which I received later for the Burma Retreat, which came out well before it. The other piece of news was that I was to be upgraded to a GSO II and to report to Army HQ, India, as soon as an air passage could be arranged. I understood that it was to a job in security in the 'Far East', but whether it was Malaya or Burma, I did not know. It was lucky that it turned out to be Burma, where I managed to keep one jump ahead of the Japs, and not Malaya, where I should have been 'in the bag'.

My 28th birthday was coming up and John Hudson organised a combined birthday and farewell dinner at the Zia Hotel. He had the brilliant idea of using the Identity Card records to find some female company. The Intelligence Officer in charge was ordered to produce the Record Cards of the Nurses working in the British Military Hospitals around Bagdad. John picked out the four best looking and invited them. They all came, but, I think, purely out of curiosity. We had a very pleasant evening and a few days later I was on a KLM flight to Karachi.

The Burma Retreat

I WENT on from Karachi to Delhi, where I was told that I was to be GSO II(Ib) of Burma Army, and was introduced to my GSO I to be, another 14th Punjabi, Philip Gwyn. We were to fly to Rangoon as soon as transport could be arranged. Philip Gwyn was a big man in every sense of the word, and although he did not suffer fools gladly, he was a very kind and considerate superior. He was eminently suitable for the job of Intelligence Chief in Burma, as he was a Japanese Interpreter, and knew more than most of the Japanese methods of making war as he had served for a while in Shanghai.

During my last month in Iraq, the War had taken a very nasty turn; the greater part of the American Pacific Fleet had been sunk at Pearl Harbour, Hong Kong had surrendered, and the Japanese had invaded Malaya, after first sinking the Repulse and Prince of Wales. I confess that all this meant very little to me at the time as I was leaving Iraq with a good report and a recommendation for a 'Mention' and was going to a new and interesting job as a second grade Staff Officer carrying the rank of Major, while I was still a substantive Lieutenant, but most of all, I had the supreme confidence that whatever setbacks the British forces might endure all would come right in the end and we would win the final battle.

I will not continue with my adventures in Burma, as they have already been described in my book 'Retreat from Burma — an Intelligence Officer's Personal Story', but just to summarise, I was Assistant Military Governor (Law and Order), in Rangoon until the bitter end and narrowly escaped capture by the

Japanese. Four Field Security Sections were raised during the campaign, all of whom did sterling work during the Retreat, but not always of a strictly security nature. I arrived back in India, in due course, to be told that I was to take ten days 'Refitting leave' and report back to Assam as a GSO II(Ib) of 4 Corps on the conclusion of my leave.

Things did not work quite like that as I was taken ill on the train and it was a month before I got back to Assam to take up my new duties. I had been asked for as the first Commandant of the new Indian Intelligence Corps, but in view of the situation in Eastern India, 4 Corps refused to release me. HQ 4 Corps had only recently arrived from England, and had been allowed to commandeer any Officer of Burma Army, so to Assam I had to go.

CHAPTER THREE

ASSAM — Gauhati Intelligence Detachment

I HEARD from Philip Gwyn, while I was on leave. Once again he was going to be my boss, as GSO I(I) of 4 Corps. The Intelligence set up in the Corps Head Quarters was being split into Operational and Lines of Communications. This was because the Corps would be responsible not only for the fighting formations on the Manipur front but also for the L of C in the Province of Assam. HQ 4 Corps was a British not an Indian HQ, although later it became so changed that it was soon indistinguishable from an Indian Corps HQ. It had arrived from the United Kingdom and had immediately been sent up to Assam, where it had set up its HQ at Jorhat. The Intelligence Staff had consisted of a GSO II, a regular, Derek Holbrook, a GSO III for I(b) work, Peter Leefe, a war time Officer of the Intelligence Corps, and two other Intelligence Officers. To this had been added, Philip Gwyn as a GSO I, myself as a GSO II and an Intelligence Officer 'Rama' Ramamirthan, all from the Intelligence Staff of Burma Army.

It had been decreed that Philip Gwyn, as the Senior Intelligence Officer would be situated in Corps HQ at Jorhat, but

an 'ad hoc' HQ would be formed at Gauhati to deal with
Security problems on the L of C. This would consist of myself
as the OC, Philip Leefe, and Rama, together with two British
Clerks. It was further decreed that we were to be provided with
a requisitioned house in which the Officers would work, eat
and sleep. I was authorised to buy crockery and cutlery and
pay for it out of the 'slush fund'.

I duly set off for Gauhati at the conclusion of my leave,
expecting a speedier and more comfortable journey than the
one I had had on leaving Assam a month or so earlier. All
went well as far as Calcultta, where I was told that, as the metre
gauge railway line along the north bank of the Brahmaputra had
been washed out, the Assam Mail would not be running beyond
the Bengal Assam border. I was advised to go 'south about',
by taking the Surma Mail to Badarpur Junction in South
Assam, and then local trains first over the 'hill section' to
Lumding and then on to Gauhati. The journey was both
comfortable and interesting as far as Lumding, as it entailed a
nine hour journey on a river steamer and a daylight trip over
the scenic hill section. My luck changed at Lumding where
chaos reigned once again and I had to finish my journey on a
local train travelling third class.

The Province was the smallest and the worst off for communications of all those comprising British India. Geographically,
it consisted of two fertile valleys, the Brahmaputra or Assam
Valley to the north and the Surma Valley to the south; between
the two lay the Khasi and Jaintia Hills rising to about 6,000
feet. It was bounded to the north by the Himalayan Range
forming the boundary with Tibet and rising to over 17,000 feet.
Mountain ranges of 10,000 feet bounded the Province on the
east and south forming the boundary with China and Burma.
Only to the west was there flat country, but the Brahmaputra,
unbridged throughout the whole of its length hindered communications with the rest of India as well as cutting the Assam
Valley in two.

Communications were very poor, and there were only three
trunk roads in the whole Province. A tarred road ran from
Gauhati on the Brahmaputra up to Shillong in the Khasi Hills

and down the other side to Sylhet, and another from Manipur Road Station via Kohima to Imphal, the capital of Manipur State. Both these roads were typical Indian 'hill' roads with sharp curves and steep gradients. They had to be operated as one way roads with traffic only being allowed to proceed in one direction over a given section. This gave them a very low traffic density. The Manipur Road was not really a trunk road as it did not connect with any other road. The other trunk road, the recently constructed Assam Trunk Road, untarred, ran from Gauhati up the Valley to Dibrugarh. There was no road communication with India proper.

The main arteries of communication were river and rail; large river steamers could proceed upstream as far as Dibrugargh, but low water in May and June usually restricted services to Gauhati only, and flood water in the monsoon season of July, August and September made navigation so hazardous that services were usually suspended.

The railways were all single line and of metre gauge. The trunk line, the Assam Bengal, was built to obviate the river passage and carry the produce of the Assam Valley to the east Bengal seaport of Chittagong. In the Assam Valley a branch ran to Gauhati where a wagon ferry connected with another metre gauge line to Bengal. Two branches in the Surma Valley ran westwards to connect with other wagon ferries. In fact, wagon ferries were the only communication with India proper.

For the purpose of Government, Assam was divided into three distinct entities. The province itself, divided into ten civil Districts, the Native States, made up of the large and homogenous State of Manipur on the Burma border and the hotch potch of tiny States in the Khasi Hills, with finally the tribal territory in the mountains around the perimeter of the Province. The States and Tribal territory were overseen by the Government of Assam's Political Department, and to keep order in the Tribal Territory, the Government maintained a very efficient para military force — the Assam Rifles — composed mainly of Gurkhas and officered almost entirely by Officers seconded from regular Gurkha Regiments.

By the time I arrived in Gauhati, the military situation was that the Japanese advance had petered out on the Indo-Burma border, largely owing to the monsoon. This was a lucky break as the troops under command of 4 Corps were very few in numbers. An Indian Division, the 23rd, of two Brigades only was already in Manipur, and it had been intended to re-equip both of the Divisions of the Burma Army there, the 17th Indian and the 1st Burma, but the supply position had become so bad that it was impossible to feed both these Divisions much less re-equip them. The difficulties on the L of C were caused by the inadequacies of the railway system, made worse by the wash out on the line from Bengal already mentioned, and, in addition, the port of Chittagong could not be used as we had lost command of the sea in the Bay of Bengal. As if this was not enough, the efforts to improve the road to Manipur had destroyed the natural drainage, and the exceptionally heavy monsoon rains had washed it down the hillside over long stretches. The decision was then taken to move 1 Bur Div to Shillong until it could be sent back to India. An attempt had been made to organise the rear areas in the Province, by setting up an Assam L of C Head Quarters at Gauhati, and the nucleus of L of C sub areas HQs at Shillong, Dibrugarh, and Manipur Road Base.

Peter Leefe and Rama Ramamirthan and our two British clerks were already in Gauhati living in the Reinforcement Camp, so the first thing was to organise ourselves, before we could tackle the security problems. The Administrative Commandant allotted us a house in the 'civil lines' opposite the Commissioner's bungalow and a short distance from the residences and offices of the District Magistrate and Superintendent of Police. The house, a bungalow was 'L' shaped: in the shorter part, which faced the road, were two rooms, one was the general office, and the other Peter Leefe's office, in the longer part was my combined office and bedroom, then two rooms for Peter and Rama and finally a room for our Mess, with a Verandah, front and back, connecting all the rooms. There was also an Annexe, containing two further rooms, which would be useful for accommodating visitors. We hired furniture and bought crockery and cutlery in the bazaar, engaged a cook and a sweeper, as, naturally, the bungalow had no main drainage. The clerks had brought office equipment and stationery from Corps HQ, so the Gauhati Intelligence Detachment of 4 Corps was open for business.

The time had now come to review the tasks and the forces available to tackle them. First the Intelligence Detachment itself; I was in a curious position, I had, I presume, the disciplinary and administrative powers of a Detachment Commander of Field rank, but I was primarily a Staff Officer of 4 Corps, charged with the security of its rear areas. I was doing this work in and for HQ Assam L of C who had no Intelligence or Security staff of their own. This was reflected in the way I signed letters; for purely local administrative matters as 'OC Int Det', to units and formations in the Corps as 'Major, General Staff' i.e. an order from the Corps Commander, and on a few rare occasions 'for Lieutenant General, GOC in C, 4 Corps'. Peter Leefe my 2 i/c had been a business man from Shanghai, who had been on leave in England in 1939, and enlisted into the Military Police's first Field Security Police section. He was evacuated from Dunkirk as a Sergeant, and on the FSP's transfer to the Intelligence Corps was commissioned into that Corps. While he had little knowledge of the Indian scene, he did have a great knowledge of security work. Rama was rather the odd man out — a South Indian Brahmin and a Professor at Rangoon University, he had been commissioned during the Burma Retreat, without any Intelligence or other training. A wonderful man in many ways, he was not a great help to us and before long he was transferred to Public Relations. Our two British clerks were from the Indian Army Corps of Clerks, a Sub Conductor and a Staff Sergeant. The remaining members of our team were my Gurkha Orderly and Peter Leefe's British batman. My orderly Naik Faudebahadur Mall had been lent me by the CO of our newly raised 5th Battalion with the idea that he would learn something about security so that on his return, he could become the Battalion Provost Havildar. Unfortunately, as a Gurkha of one of the highest clans in the Nepal social order, he did not shine either as an orderly or in security work, so in due course I replaced him by a Gurkha civilian servant. Peter Leefe's batman was a Private of the Royal Engineers, who appears to have sunk to the level of a member of HQ 4 Corps' Employment Platoon through drink. In due course he had to go as well. However when sober, he was one of the best servants, that I have known. These four lived and fed in the Reinforcement Camp. An Assamese youth whom Peter Leefe's batman had recruited as a pantry boy and general servant completed the team; while not particularly bright he was cheerful and willing and answered to the shout of 'Nuts', his real name being 'Nath'.

Although we had now a good management team, our resources on the ground were meagre for such a large area, especially one which was quickly filling up with Depots and other L of C organisations, and through which ran the main artery on which the forward troops depended. There were originally only two Field Security Sections in the Province, No 25 (British) which had come from the UK with 4 Corps Headquarters, and an all Indian Section designated for 26 Indian Division, This later section had never reached the Division but was sitting in Manipur Road base doing nothing as the FSO had been evacuated as a mental case. No 25 was one of the original sections of the British Intelligence Corps, highly trained and similar to those which I have already described in Chapter III. It was ineffective as neither the FSO nor any of the men had any knowledge of the Indian scene, nor was there anyone as yet to direct them.

An unexpected and very welcome reinforcement came with the arrival of two of my Burma FSOs, Summersell and Acomb, with the better part of their sections, Nos 2 and 4 Burma. Their arrival was due to the loyalty of these two Officers, particularly Summersell, and the good offices of my old friend and Commandant, at Karachi, Jock Campbell. Summersell had heard that I had been appointed to Assam and went and told Jock that they wantd to go there, as he was sure that I would be short of personnel and would welcome them. Jock very naturally said that he had no authority to send sections to the other end of

India, and anyway Army HQ and the Government of Burma would have to be consulted. However Summersell was so insistent that finally Jock gave way and packed off the two sections without any proper authority; an action for which I was very grateful.

It was fortunate that I was a staff officer of HQ 4 Corps and that Philip Gwyn was my boss, otherwise there would have been trouble both in my absorbing two Burma sections and also for the break up of sections and re-distribution of their personnel. Philip Gwyn agreed with my suggestions that the forward troops could look after themselves and that our efforts should be concentrated on the Base and L of C units; a policy that I had initiated in Iraq and Burma. We pooled all the men, British and Indian and by re-distribution were able to form four reasonable sections, which were stationed at Manipur Road Base, Dibrugarh, Silchar and Gauhati, Acomb went to Silchar, but I chose Summersell, specially for the section at Manipur Road, as I considered this the most important. About this time the distinction between the all Indian Divisional section and the composite L of C section was abolished; all sections in the future were to be composite. Shortly afterwards all sections based on Karachi were put onto a common numerical roll from 550 onwards, so the old titles of 26 Div Section or 2 Burma ceased to exist. As a concession, two sections were given the title 'Burma' after their name; this was given to No 2, but not to No 4 as by mistake this title was given to a Karachi raised section. I should mention here our only Burmese Field Security NCO, Havildar Saw William, a Christian Karen, who had come out of Burma with his section and now had arrived in Assam. He was extremely efficient and westernised, so he attached himself to the British half of his section, acquired a British Other Rank's peaked cap, and was normally known as Sergeant Williams. Later he requested re-enlistment as a British Rank on the grounds that he was doing a British Rank's work. In spite of a strong recommendation from Philip Gwyn, this was turned down by the Government of Burma (in exile) as an undesirable precedent. Saw Williams's request was not so unusual, as I found out later that Christian Karens were enlisted as British Ranks in the Burma Auxiliary Force, provided the European and Anglo Indian personnel agreed.

My time in Assam from July 1942 to September 1943 can be divided into two phases; the first coincided with my time in the Gauhati Intelligence Detachment and lasted until the spring of 1943, the second came when the detachnent had been absorbed into the Headquarters of No 202 L of C Area and I had become the Chief Intelligence Officer of that Area. The first period was both the most challenging and also the most interesting; as in Iraq we were starting from scratch as far as unit security was concerned but instead of counter espionage work on the Iraq railways, we were involved in counter sabotage on those in Assam. The second period was more concerned with routine, as I was now responsible for all forms of Intelligence and had a GSO III and an IO for operational intelligence, mainly communications, as well as Peter Leefe and the Security staff.

None of the units in or arriving in Assam had had any Security training and the position was made worse by the fact, that, incredible as it may seem, India Command had still not issued Officer's Identity Cards, although we were assured that this was in hand and the issue was likely to begin in the autumn. What was more serious was the lack of Security Authority Cards, essential for FS personnel if they were to carry out their functions. Identity Cards could wait, but the others could not, so with Philip Gwyn's approval, we had them printed at the Government Security Press at Calcutta, and paid for out of the 'slush' fund. They had the standard wording authorising the bearer to 'be in any place, at any time, in any dress in the execution of his duty' and calling on all military personnel to render him every assistance. These I signed 'for and on behalf of the GOC in C, 4 Corps'. My own Card, No 1, is in the Intelligence Corps Museum at Ashford, and is probably the only specimen of such a Card issued by a lower formation such as a Corps HQ. Much later such Cards were issued by the Indian Intelligence Corps Depot at Karachi on behalf of India Command.

Before we had time to get started on any security work, we had to deal with the dislocation caused on the political front and, in particular, the '42' rebellion. The British Government had sent out a Mission in the early spring of 1942 led by Sir Stafford Cripps, to try to get the Indian National Congress to support the war effort. Their reply was — only if India was granted immediate self government; a proposal which was not acceptable with the Japanese knocking at India's door. The Congress then proceeded to plan a massive civil disobedience campaign; even Gandhi, the apostle of non-violence, stated that — while the burning of Government Offices, Police Stations and Banks was not permissible, the destruction of railway permanent way, stations, bridges and other communications was, provided it was done in a 'non-violent' manner and ample precautions had been taken to safeguard life.

The Congress decided on the 8th August to start their campaign, and the Government countered on the next day by a massive round up of the Congress leaders, both national and local. There was a lull for two days and, then, on the 11th, all hell broke lose. Violent rioting took place in nearly every major city of India, and this took the form of attempts to burn and loot government and railway property. Serious damage was done before order was restored a day or so later.

There were further outbreaks in the country side, which were particularly severe in the Madras and Bombay Presidencies, the western part of Bengal, the UP, Bihar and the Central Provinces — attacks were made on railway stations and communications generally — and the situation was not brought under control for some two or three weeks, but, except in the eastern UP and Bihar the civil authorities never lost complete control of their districts.

The most serious outbreak occurred in the eastern part of the UP and western Bihar. The pattern of the disturbances was the same; a mass uprising over the whole countryside with attacks on anything which could be called Government property. Post Offices were looted and burnt; Police Stations were attacked and at the height of the trouble only some three Stations out of a District total of about twenty remained in

Government hands, and as a result, by about the 14th of August, Government control and law and order had ceased to exist outside the District Headquarter towns. Complete order was not restored nor rail communications reopened until about four or five week's had elapsed.

Trouble did not erupt in Assam until about two weeks later, and when it did come it was minor compared with the troubles in the UP and Bihar. I had hoped that trouble would pass us by, except perhaps for some processions and 'Quit India' demonstrations. This was because Assam had never been a Congress stronghold, and there was a sizeable Moslem minority, indeed, on the Congress withdrawing from Government in 1939, the Moslem League had formed a Ministry, which was still in office.

I was wrong, trouble did come and two incidents were reported. The first was on the railway line on the north bank of the Brahmaputra, still out of action on account of the washouts mentioned earlier. Mobs approached the railway repair gangs and frightened away the labour. The second was serious rioting, with some damage to property in the town of Nowgong on the Assam Trunk road some miles north east to Gauhati. In normal times and in most Provinces, such disturbances would not have merited calling out the troops, but would have been dealt with by armed Police but things were different at this time in Assam. The Province had relied previously on the Assam Rifles to do this sort of police work, but now the reserve capacity of this Force was on the Burma border.

The Government of Assam naturally turned to the Army for assistance, but they were in no better case, HQ Assam L of C could dispose of practically no fighting troops, only a large number of Base and L of C units. The only possible force was a British Battalion from the Burma Army in Shillong, and the Indian soldiers in the Gauhati Reinforcement camp. The former, which was sorting itself out after the Retreat, was under strength, lacking in Officers and equipment and of poor morale; the latter was a collection of soldiers, mostly recruits from different units lacking in everything necessary for service; arms, equipment, Officers and NCOs. However something had to be done and I was summoned to a conference at L of C HQ. I knew the General, Eric Goddard, well as he had been our Brigade Commander in Landi Kotal, when I was on 'notice' and I had acted as his Brigade Orderly Officer on a frontier 'column'. Later I met him on the Burma Retreat as he was the Burma Army's Major General, Administration. He was extremely energetic and efficient, but very highly strung, and did not suffer fools gladly; indeed, many considered him very brutal to his subordinates, but I had always got on very well with him. His senior General Staff Officer, Malcolm McGill was from my own battalion.

The plan decided on was to bring down a Company of the British Battalion from Shillong, take it over the Ferry to Amingaon on the north bank, from whence a special train would convey it to the scene of the trouble. It would then be split up between two or three stations to deal with any trouble that might arise. The General travelled over on the Ferry and during the passage he gave his opinion, in no uncertain terms, as to the efficiency of the company and the competence of the Officers. I had taken the precaution to send Peter Leefe with them as an Intelligence observer, and it was a good thing that I did, as he had more or less to get the men to their posts as the Officers were quite useless, and the only man who had any notion of what to do was the Company Sergeant Major. Their presence, however, prevented any further interference with the repair work.

There was an amusing sequel to this: the General, a week or so later wished to inspect this company, so a special train was laid on again, and I was asked to come, together with the District Magistrate, Superintendent of Police and the appropriate Railway Officers. Eric Goddard was not satisfied with what he saw, and proceeded to hand out rebukes to all and sundry. Almost at the end of the inspection, he met the Medical Officer, and asked 'Is there anything you want, Doctor?' The immediate reply was 'I would like some ice'. The General let out a bellow 'what do you want ice for?', and we all expected that the MO's reply would occasion another blast, but he replied sweetly 'It is always worth asking'. This completely floored Eric, who then became almost human.

An old friend of mine and colleague at Sandhurst, 'Shorty' ffinch of the 4th Gurkhas was sent off to Nowgong with a composite company of Gurkhas from the Reinforcement Camp. His exploits are best described in the words of the District Magistrate 'As soon as Captain ffinch got here, I knew he meant business'. There was no more trouble in that District.

We had a further disturbance on the railway, this time between Gauhati and Lumding Junction. There had been a derailment, and the authorities were running passenger trains up to the scene from both sides and transhipping passengers and luggage across the gap. I heard from the Railway Transport Officer at Gauhati that there had been trouble up the line and he had stopped all military passengers from travelling on the up Mail train, which nevertheless left normally. Shortly afterwards HQ Assam L of C received a request for troops, who had to be hastily got together from the Reinforcement Camp for dispatch by special train to the scene of the trouble. This time I decided to see for myself what the trouble was, taking with me as a bodyguard, a Sergeant from the Gauhati FS Section.

The train proceeded normally until two stations before the break; here the Stationmaster informed us that he was getting no reply to his 'line clear' requests. We had to go on, line clear or no line clear, so the driver was instructed to proceed with great caution, sounding his whistle at intervals; the danger was that the Mail might be halted 'in section', and we would run into it. All was well, however, and we duly came to a halt at the Home Signal of the next station, which was 'At Danger'. Nothing came of our repeated whistles, so a section of troops were detrained, and sent forward to secure the station; when they had done this, they were to lower the signal and our train would come in.

We went forward in due course and pulled into a deserted, but undamaged station, where the up Mail train was still standing. After a while the Stationmaster appeared and told us what had happened — a disorderly mob had roamed about the village frightening all and sundry, with the Police making no attempt to disperse them. The station staff had decamped, the Stationmaster locking himself in his quarters. After a while the mob made off up the line to the break. There they met an Anglo Indian Assistant Engineer, whom they took for a European, and shouted at him to 'Go home'. He replied, with some wit, 'why, I am an Indian', they then made him don a 'Gandhi Cap' and shout 'Gandhiji ke Jai' (Victory to the noble Gandhi), after which they dispersed without doing any damage. They had frightened off, of course, the railway labour.

It was decided to leave a military post at the station and at the break to reassure the railway staff, and also to move the Mail up to where the down Mail was waiting on the other side. My work done, I decided to return by the Mail, which would leave as soon as the transhipment had been completed. It was now late evening, and my companion and I were decidedly hungry; the Assam Mail was one of the few metre gauge trains with a Dining Car, so I hailed the Anglo Indian train Conductor and asked if there was any dinner ready, and got the cheerful reply 'Of course Sir, roast duck'. The Sergeant and I had a good meal and then lay down on the bunks of a I class compartment, I confess I was a little uneasy until we reached Chaparmukh Junction, where the engine could be turned as we were running tender first, without a headlight, on unfenced track, where animals abounded, to say nothing of a possible attempt at derailment by the disaffected. We slept peacefully, however, and duly arrived back at Gauhati.

This was the end of any disturbances sufficiently serious for troops to be called out, but complete law and order was far from re-established over the whole Province. Railway sabotage became a great problem, not by mobs, but by derailments caused by malicious damage to the track; special measures were introduced later to combat this. Occasionally some black humour surfaced; it was reported that a shunting engine in Pandu Yard had blown up, killing the crew, and the other crews were refusing duty fearing that explosives had been hidden in the coal. This hold up of movement was extremely serious, so I went personally to investigate. The first thing that

I noticed was that, except that the cab was missing, the engine appeared completely undamaged. This ruled out any explosion in the firebox, so we were able to reassure the crews who returned to work. The dead men had been blown a considerable distance by the force of the explosion, and near the bodies were wood fragments which looked as if they had been part of a packing case. Further investigation found a wagon broken into, and this contained blasting powder. The mystery was now solved; the engine crew, obviously, had been in the habit of pilfering, and had mistaken a case of blasting powder for canned food. This they had tried to open on the footplate and, of course, it had exploded.

The absence of any military or para military force to carry out the complete restoration of law and order in the remoter parts of the country side, led to an odd situation. While the towns and the railway and roads were firmly held, the remoter areas were for the time being left alone; so the local Congress leaders made an unofficial bargain with local officialdom. The Magistrates were in their Courts, and the Police in their Stations, but no cases were tried, no revenue was collected, and no police investigations carried out. In return, the Congress leaders refrained from attacking Government servants or property.

During this time I was kept busy meeting the local civil and police authorities. Philip Gwyn came down from Corps HQ at Jorhat to discuss our problems and we went up to Shillong to consult with the Chief Secretary to Government and with the Inspector General of Police and the Deputy Inspector General in charge of the CID. We had intended to motor up by the afternoon 'gate' (convoy), but before we had even reached the half way point where the up and down convoys passed each other, our decrepit requisitioned car broke down, and we had to return to Gauhati and go up on the following day by public transport. This may have been a blessing in disguise as Philip, on his return to Jorhat, persuaded Ordnance to issue us with a brand new Chevrolet station wagon.

I found that a new dimension was necessary in GSI(b) work in the Indian theatre. As India was a British possession there was no Civil Affairs staff as would have been found in Libya or Italy, because the normal peace time administration was in being. The GSI(b) staff had, of necessity, close liaison with the civil authorities so in time it became quite usual to use them for liaison in many matters, not necessarily of a security nature. This close liaison was even more necessary as in areas where the normal civil administration functioned, as Army security personnel had no special rights or privileges. The Defence of Burma Rules had had a clause which allowed the Army Commander to delegate certain police powers to me, but I think that the Defence of India Rules had no such clause, certainly I was never given any such powers. The Inspector General of Police smoothed over these difficulties by instructing all District Superintendents to co-operate to the full with us, and, further, he deputed an Inspector to be part of the Gauhati Intelligence Detachment.

Another area where there was a difference to other theatres was corruption and this was a real headache. Corruption is endemic in the East, and while it had been kept in check in peace time, the war time expansion had allowed it to reach formidable proportions. Dealing with this was not our job, but often it came to light in security investigations. In other theatres, it would have been handed over to the Special Investigation Branch of the Military Police, but there were none such in India at that time, and there was a great shortage of any Military Police — to have done nothing would have got us a bad name, so reluctantly we were forced to take action.

A case occurred where I had to deal with the civil authorities on the highest level in connection with 'Aid to the Civil Power'. The District Magistrate had asked for troops to help arrest a notorious malefactor who was terrorising the countryside. A squad of Gurkhas, under a very young and inexperienced British Officer, was sent, together with an Indian Magistrate of the 3rd Class. He, alone, as representing the Civil Power could authorise the use of force. The man was duly run to earth in his village and cornered in a hut, where he took up a belligerent attitude. The Magistrate then ordered the troops to open fire. This was quite wrong, as he had no authority to do this only to order the Officer to use such *force as was necesary* to effect an arrest. Fire was opened and the man went down wounded. So far all was well and the Magistrate's lapse had done little harm, but unfortunately as the villain continued his belligerence the Magistrate to use his own words 'ordered for the bayonet charging', which was done and the man died of his wounds. The Civil authorities then completely lost their heads. It was an axiom that the bayonet was never used in aid to the civil power and, in any event, to bayonet a wounded man was entirely against the principle of minimum or necessary force. They started to talk wildly about starting criminal proceedings against the Officer and he for his part boasted of what he had done, instead of keeping his mouth shut.

In actual fact, under the Code of Criminal Procedure no action could be taken without the sanction of the Governor General in Council. Both men were to blame, but in my opinion, the Magistrate was the most at fault. Although he was a Magistrate with limited powers, he should have known the law which only allowed him to authorise the use of force; how much and what kind of force was entirely the responsibility of the Commander of the troops. The Officer of course, was at fault in obeying the improper instruction that he had been given. The whole affair appeared likely to blow up into a major civil-military row, so the General asked me to try and cool matters down. I considered that the best plan was to go direct to the Commissioner of the Division, rather than the District Magistrate. He started on a high tone but I reminded him that the most part of the blame was attributable to the Magistrate, and I would advise the GOC in C, 4 Corps to make a formal complaint to the Government of India through Army HQ. After a while, he calmed down and on my assurance that the Officer would get a severe rebuke he agreed that the best thing was to let the matter drop.

Once we had got over the repercussions of the '42 rebellion, it might have been thought that we should be able to get down to our proper work of 'securing' the L of C, but not so, yet again we were told off to do a job for which we were not really equipped or organised. This was the organisation of temporary detention camps for refugees from Burma. The first wave of

Indian refugees had come in advance of the Burma Army, and, therefore, had not been in contact with the Japanese, but many had been held up by the monsoon and had continued their journey in October long after the Japanese had occupied the whole country. It was possible that these latter parties might have been infiltrated by Japanese agents. It was decided, therefore, that all such should be checked and, if necessary, interrogated before being allowed to pass into India proper. A number of agencies were involved; Army HQ provided the Interpreters and Interrogators, the Army built the camps, the Assam Police guarded them and kept order, but the Gauhati Intelligence Detachment was the co-ordinator, and had to find and direct the refugees to the Camps. Once again, in other Theatres, much of this would have been the job of the Military Police or Civil Affairs staff, but these did not exist in Assam, so it was the Field Security Sections, who had to do the job.

I must admit that my heart sank when I considered the difficulties and the paucity of the resources available, but there were two factors acting in our favour — financial and geographical. Many of the refugees had considerable sums of money with them. Burma used Indian currency, but the Rupee notes issued by the Reserve Bank of India for use within Burma, had their numbers in red instead of the usual black. These notes were not usually accepted in India but in normal times could be exchanged at a Bank at par and without any formality. The Government passed an Order under the Defence of India Rules prohibiting Banks from exchanging such notes without an authorisation from one of the Interrogation Camps. This was a great incentive for the refugees to go voluntarily into the Camps, and certainly facilitated some aspects of our work, but the physical side the actual listing of the notes and comparing them with a 'black list' put a great strain on the Field Security personnel available.

No one could come from Burma to India proper, without crossing the unbridged Brahmaputra River by one of the relatively few Ferries. As we were concerned only with the Province of Assam, this meant that we had only one to watch, the rail ferry between Pandu and Amigaon two or three miles west of

Gauhati. Bus services, except on a few routes being almost non existent, we were concerned mainly with the two daily trains, the Mail and the Passenger, both of which connected with trains to Calcutta on the other side of the river.

The check was carried out at Pandu and to facilitate this we had fencing erected to canalise passengers onto the Jetty; one for military and one for civilian passengers. There was also a holding pen. Naturally we concentrated on the civilians, although the other gangway was used by the Movement Control staff to check travel documents. We had to adopt very rough and ready methods, and I wonder now if we really achieved anything; the actual check was carried out by one or two British and Indian FS NCOs, with a civil policeman in attendance. The modus operandi was to allow anyone one looking like an Assamese or a Bengali to pass through and to check all others. There was only time for a few quick questions — 'Where do you come from? — Where do you work? — Where did you board the train?' and so on. Anyone whose answers did not ring true was put back into the pen for a later and more detailed questioning; if we were not satisfied, the man was arrested by the civil police and removed to the Camp, where a Magistrate passed a temporary detention order on him.

The check was taken off by November as there appeared to be no more refugees coming through. This was a great relief to us as it allowed the Field Security personnel to get on with their proper tasks of security education of units and advising on the physical security of military installations. The fencing remained in position, however, and was much used later by the Military Police in checking the documents of Military personnel. The civilian gangway came into its own again, when the Japanese started to parachute agents into Assam.

The Railway had been repaired and was carrying a very heavy traffic, both inward and outward. Into the area came fresh troops, together with the enormous tonnage of military stores of all sorts bound for the huge depot at Manipur Road Station. Outward traffic was the movement back to India of the remnants of the Burma Army, who had been held up by the breaches on the line. Further outward traffic was caused by the movement of three Chinese Armies (actually each was no bigger than a British Division), who had originally been in Burma and were on their way to Ramgarh in Bihar for re-organisation and re-equipping.

Measures were in hand to improve the railways within Assam but the carrying capacity was still very low, caused by the long haul over poorly equipped metre gauge lines, with the bottle neck of the Amigaon-Pandu wagon ferry. It was essential that there were no other hold ups, otherwise it was possible that the forward troops would have to be put on reduced rations. A spate of derailments caused by sabotage occurred, which made the protection of the line a first priority. This was not going to be easy, as there were several hundred miles of main line and, as yet no troops allotted for its protection. Fortunately the railway men, particularily the Anglo Indian Drivers were stout hearted and continued to drive trains through the night in spite of the danger.

I went out to the scene of one incident where the engine of a troop train had gone down the embankment, taking the first vehicle a, luggage van, with it. The engine had rolled over the Driver, the poor fellow was not a pretty sight.

Originally when the derailments started there was some doubt as to the reason, and the local Press and Politicians made a great stir that it was due to poor maintenance and excessive traffic. There was a reason for this — if it could be proved that it was sabotage, the Railway Administration would not be liable to pay compensation to the victims of the accident. I had taken some Field Security NCOs with me to the scene of the derailment, more as a training exercise than anything else. I explained that they were there to try and determine the cause of the accident and not to help the railway personnel nor the injured, but to search the vicinity for any clues. We were lucky that we found a fishplate thrown into the undergrowth, together with a its bolt which a tidy minded saboteur had put through its hole and then threaded the nut on. This proved sabotage without any doubt.

It was never established whether this activity was Japanese inspired, or purely the work of local disaffecteds, or a combination of the two. Whatever it was, it was very serious; India started the War with little spare capacity in locomotives or rolling stock nor did she manufacture them. Neither Britain her, traditional supplier, nor America could help without damage to their respective war efforts. This meant that the railway authorities has to make an agonising decision, whether to merely roll the derailed stock off the track and resume traffic or to try and recover it, often from the bottom of a high embankment, which might close the line for several days.

It was obvious that something had to be done, but what? Troops were still scarce, and needed in the forward areas, while the amount of line which would have to be patrolled was very considerable. Excluding one or two unimportant branch lines, the railway mileage, within the Province amounted to some six hundred miles. However, this could be divided up into those lines absolutely vital to the war effort and those not so vital. These categories could be subdivided again into those lines most likely to be sabotaged and those less likely.

The port of Chittagong was unuseable as a result of enemy activity in the Bay of Bengal, so the bulk of the military traffic had to come from inside India, and the route along the Assam Valley would have to bear by far the heaviest traffic. This involved a mileage of 308 miles — 146 miles along the north bank to the Amigaon-Pandu ferry, 118 miles on the Gauhati Branch and finally 44 miles of the main line to Manipur Road base. The other route was from wagon ferries in Bengal, along the Surma Valley and over the 'hill section' to join the main line at Lumding giving a total of 136 miles, of which the hill section accounted for 115 miles. There was a third route of considerable but not vital importance, the prolongation of the main line from Manipur Road to Dibrugarh; this served the staging Airfields of the American-China route in North Assam, as well as the Digboi Oilfield and the Ledo Coal Mines, giving a total of 170 miles.

I assessed that the most dangerous sections would be those where the line ran in jungle giving cover right up to the actual line. The section from Gauhati to Manipur Road and a short distance farther on fell into this category. The 'Hill Section' was thick jungle with many vulnerable tunnels, but it was not a vital line and, further, it was in tribal territory, where the local inhabitants could easily spot a stranger. In addition, it was patrolled by a tribal force, the 'North Cachar Hills Watch and Ward' organised by an anthropologist, Miss Ursula Graham Bower, as a part of the famous 'V' Force which had been formed to watch out for enemy agents and infiltrators. The remainder of the lines ran in cultivated areas, where a group bent on evil could easily be spotted.

The plan finally decided on was a three tier system. First, the Assam Government issued orders that the villages adjacent to the line must patrol it, under threat of collective fines. Second, the Inspector General of Police undertook to raise a force of about 1000 Auxiliary Police, mostly from Gurkhas domiciled in the Province. There would be a detachment at every station in the dangerous areas and at others less vulnerable, from where they would patrol and keep the village protection parties up to the mark. They were given the code name 'Railforce'. The final tier was an Indian Territorial Battalion, code name 'Railtroops', having their HQ at Lumding, the focal point, with company detachments at Gauhati, and other important railway centres; the Commanding Officer was made responsible for the efficient working of the whole scheme.

Railforce was to be equipped on the simplest scale, merely a khaki shirt and shorts, with a rifle and 5 rounds of ammunition, and, of course the inevitable 'Kukri' which the individual provided himself. The Government of Assam had neither stocks of clothing nor arms, so these had to be provided from Army sources, and once again it was the Gauhati Intelligence Detachment who had to act as the co-ordinaters.

There was an amusing and unforeseen twist to this: the Police, of all people wished to know who would be providing the opium?. Assam was very badly malaria ridden, indeed, in and around Manipur Road Station an extremely virulent strain of cerebral malaria was found, which was usually fatal. The locals were in the habit of taking opium as a prophylatic, and without it, it was more than probable that half the force would be inoperative. I am afraid I cannot remember who actually provided the drug.

There was another problem of sabotage distinct from derailments, but luckily it was confined to a small section of the line. The Gauhati Branch had the lowest permissible form of signalling, Class 3, and the North bank line was little better. Class 3 did not involve complicated interlocking of points and signals, but merely hand operated points and signals worked by a winch or even a lever at the signal post, so it was not easy to do any lasting damage; even if the signals were destroyed, a pointsman with a flag or lamp sitting on the point lever would do equally well. However the Assam Bengal Railway, had resignalled Lumding and Badurpur Junctions with electrically operated colour light signals and electric point motors, together with a complicated system of interlocked double wire signals and points at the stations between Lumding and Manipur Road. These two systems were relatively easy to sabotage. A fairly minor explosion at or near the lever frame of an interlocked station would cause chaos; it would be possible to operate the points manually, but this would be a great labour, as the gear would have to be disconnected, and after the points had been moved over by hand, they would have to be re bolted to prevent them moving during the passage of a train. This disruption occurred twice to my knowledge, during the Burma Retreat — on one occasion a near miss during an air raid distorted the rodding and this caused a very serious hold up. The position was potentially more serious at Lumding, where not only was there the danger of sabotage of the signal box and its 'all electric' frame, but also the possibility of interruption of the electric supply from the railway's power house. I had first hand experience of this during a visit to Lumding. I happened to be in the signal box, when there was a power failure lasting about thirty minutes. All movement came to a halt. No trains could be dispatched, no shunting could be carried out nor could any engines be got out of the Shed. My fears were groundless, however, neither sabotage nor bombing disrupted Lumding.

Early in 1942 the operating contract of the Assam Bengal Railway had expired, and the Government of India had amalgamated it with the State operated East Bengal Railway, which already owned the north bank line. This meant that all the lines in Assam were now managed from Calcutta, but as Calcutta was a long way from Assam, a semi independent administration was set up in Gauhati. A very senior railway Officer, a Mr. Hussain from the East Bengal, became Deputy General Manager. He was most helpful and co-operative, but it took him some time to understand the very backward working prevalent on parts of the Assam Bengal.

This led to a minor clash over the patrols of Railtroops and Railforce. There were only two passenger trains a day on the Gauhati Branch and the Main Line, and of these the Mail did not stop at every station, so the Administration was requested to allow the Patrols to stop good trains and ride in the brake vans to and from the areas, which they intended to patrol. This was very unpopular with the railway staff, who thought that it would hinder their pilfering, which was rife at this time. They told Mr. Hussain a cock and bull story about the delays which such a procedure would cause. I endeavoured to convince him of the absolute necessity of this if we were to combat sabotage. During the course of the interview, he said 'Of course Major, you do not understand railway working. You see to stop a goods train, the outer home signal would have to be at danger, then the train would have to be stopped at the inner home and again at the station, and the delay would be intolerable'. My reply was that this might be necessary at interlocked stations on the East Bengal, but the Gauhati Branch was Class 3 signalled, with no starting signals, and even the Mail was not allowed to run through a station at more than 5 mph, as the Driver has to watch out for the Token for the section ahead. Mr. Hussain then gave me a sweet smile and said 'I see that you know to much' and issued the necessary instructions. He very kindly gave me a written authority that all Railway staff should give me all necessary assistance, and, further, he issued to the Intelligence Detachment, three 1st Class passes for the lines in Assam and to and from Calcutta. The latter I found very useful when I went on leave.

Not long after this, I thought it would be a good idea if I took a look to see how the protection scheme was working, so I persuaded the District Traffic Superintendent, Pandu Yard, to lend me a 4 wheeled Officer's saloon. These Saloons were designed to enable railway Officers to live 'out on the line' in places were there was no suitable accommodation. The vehicles varied from the commodious bogie saloons of the senior officers to the 4 wheelers provided for junior staff such as Assistant Traffic Superintendents or Engineers. What was common to all was a bedroom, toilet compartment, kitchen and servants accommodation. DTS Pandu had provided me with an East Bengal saloon which had a longer wheel base and was better fitted up than an Assam Bengal vehicle such as I borrowed for a later inspection. My saloon had at one end a combined bedroom and office, along a corridor was the bathroom, with basin and WC, then the kitchen with a coal burning stove, fitted up with kitchen utensils, crockery and cutlery, and finally the servants compartment with an Indian type latrine; electric light and fans were fitted. I decided to inspect the most vital part of the line, that is from Gauhati to Lumding, where I should be able to contact OC Railtroops and then go on to spend a day or so inspecting Summersell's section and the security conditions at the Manipur Road Base. From there I should go back to Lumding and then over the 'Hill Section' to Badurpur Junction and on to Silcher to see Acomb and his section. I confess that I had an ulterior motive for the second part of my journey, which was to see the spectacular engineering works between Lumding and Badurpur; this was nearly my undoing.

My tour had gone very well; I had met my old friends from the Burma Retreat, Summersell and Acomb, discussed their problems with them, and as a result had learnt a great deal about my 'manor' and, also about the railway security aspect. I had reached Badurpur Junction with my saloon attached to the rear of the daily passenger train to Lumding, awaiting the train's departure for my return to Gauhati. The engine gave a whistle and off went the train leaving me behind; the saloon having been cut off. A Train Examiner now came up and told me that my saloon was 'unfit to run', and on being pressed gave the reason, the wheelbase was too long for the 'hill section'. All my arguments that it had come over safely from

Lumding being of no avail, I was advised to see the District Traffic Superintendent. I found him in his office, closeted with the District Mechanical Engineer.

This was a lucky break as the DTS, an Indian was inclined to stick by the letter of the law, while the DME was much more flexible. I told my story laying great stress on the fact that I was engaged in looking after the security of their railway. I also mentioned that the loan of the saloon and its use was very much on an old boy basis, and if the saloon could not be got back, or had to be worked back by a detour of a hundred miles or more over two wagon ferries there would be a row with reports demanded by the railway authorities in Calcutta and my friend the DTS Pandu might well be in trouble.

After some discussion, the DTS turned to his colleague and said 'we cannot risk a derailment in one of the tunnels, but is there any real danger if we take precautions — the saloon got here alright'. The DME agreed, and it was decided to send it back after the rear brake van of a goods train with another manned brake van behind to control it: so I got back without mishap.

Naturally, while all this was going on the ordinary work of the detachment proceeded under the able direction of Peter Leefe. We now had reasonable Field Security cover, and the security education of units was going ahead well. Peter started a course for unit security Officers; we put together a fake Identity Card, with Hitler's photograph cut from a magazine on it and tried it out during one of these courses; it was amazing how many units fell into the trap. It was going to be uphill job to get the average Indian soldier to check passes and Identity documents properly.

We were now well established in Gauhati, which might be described as typical of an Indian town, which had no garrison, but was the Headquarters of both a civil and a railway District. There was the usual bazaar, then down on the river bank were the Civil lines, containing the residences of the Magistrates and Police Officers with the District Courts, Police Office and Jail. In this area was a small Club, with a library, of which we made great use. The residence of the Commissioner of the Assam

Valley civil Division was situated here. Since the amalgamation of the Assam Valley Division with that of the Surma Valley, this Officer had become the 'Commissioner of Divisions'. There was also a sizeable colony of Anglo Indian railway drivers, firemen and minor officials living near the station. The town boasted a certain amount of commercial activity, mainly because Gauhati was the roadhead for the Provincial capital, Shillong: both the Indian General Navigation and British American Tobacco Companies had resident European Agents.

We got on very well with Mr. Das, Indian Civil Service, the District Magistrate, and Hewitt, the Superintendent of Police, the latter was a refugee from Burma, who had been drafted into Assam to reinforce the sparse provincial cadre. The BATS agent was a especially friendly and often invited us to his bungalow, but, unfortunately before long he was commissioned as a Staff captain in 'V' Force and left. The Steamer Agent was a somewhat cantankerous Scot, who looked upon the Army's arrival as a great nuisance.

Assam had become the rear area of the forces defending India, but this had not made much impression on Gauhati. There were few actual troops in the town, other than the Reinforcement Camp and the office of the Administrative Commandant; HQ Assam L of C was established some four miles away close to the Pandu-Amigaon Ferry, which was the main centre of activity, and, in view of the vital importance of the Ferry as a main artery of communication, a Heavy Anti Aircraft Regiment was deployed in the area. A rudimentary system of early warning had been established, and sirens had been erected in the town as well as near the Ferry. This was a great nuisance to us as the sirens were not connected to any central control, but had to be sounded by someone on the spot on the receipt of a warning over the civil telephone. The Administrative Commandant found that our Detachment was the only military unit in or near the Civil Lines, and had the Siren put in our compound for us to operate.

It was unfortunate that the primitive radar in use could not differentiate between friend and foe, and during the monsoon season all aircraft flew out of sight above the clouds. The

American aircraft bound for their airfields in Northam Assam normally flew over Gauhati, so we were perpetually operating the siren and giving up our work to go into our slit trench. This became such a nuisance, that use of 'Red' alerts for any aircraft was abandoned — luckily the Japanese left us alone. The Hy A. A. Regiment, posed another problem as it was a Territorial Army unit from Northern Ireland; the personnel, at the outbreak of war, had been embodied to serve for a fixed term. This did not apply to TA units from Britain, as they could be made to serve on under the conscription laws, but there was no conscription for residents of Northern Ireland — would these men have to be repatriated when their time was up?. I remember sending off urgent letters to HQ 4 Corps on the matter, but the men concerned patriotically agreed to waive any rights that they might have had.

There were many troops passing through Assam and in their wake came a number of Intelligence organisations, some very 'hush-hush' and controlled from outside India. Two of these we knew well: V Force, the ad hoc formation formed to stop infiltrators from Burma, and the other Z Force, set up to gather intelligence of Japanese moves close to the front line and manned mostly by European and Anglo Burmese refugees — civil servants, police and forest officers. The others were so secret that they would have nothing to do with such a lowly body as GSI (b), and in many cases their senior officers seemed to have been chosen because they knew nothing about India. This naturally caused trouble in the long run.

The first incident occurred at Manipur Road. Summersell telephoned that the had caught two alleged spies. It appeared that his braves had picked up two rather low type Anglo Burmese found wandering about the Base, who when asked to give an account of themselves, stated that they were trying to find the bus to Imphal, the Capital of Manipur State, and, now nearly in the front line. This in itself was suspicous as civilian scheduled bus services had not been running for some months, and, further, no one who was not a local was allowed into Manipur State, even in peace time, without the permission of the Political Agent. They were arrested, and when interrogated produced voluntarily codes and other documents which convinced Summersell that they were up to no good. We, in Gauhati, were not entirely happy about these two, so we instructed him to bring the pair down to Gauhati but to treat them gently. As soon as we examined their documents, it was as we had feared, Summersell had arrested two of our own agents. In his defence, their behaviour had been stupid in the extreme, but how much was their fault and how much the fault of their masters was a matter for conjecture. We packed them off back to Calcutta and a crestfallen FSO, Summersell, returned to Manipur Road. I though it prudent to send a full report to Philip Gwyn at HQ 4 Corps.

It was not long before the storm broke. Furious signals came from Calcutta and even from Britain. We were accused of every sort of ill behaviour, notably hindering the work of the secret organisation and threatening its personnel. The whole matter went up to the GOC in C, General Scoones. Here we had a champion, the General, although a difficult man in many ways, had been Director of Military Intelligence in Delhi before the war, and provided they were efficient had a soft spot for Intelligence Staffs. He said forcibly that so long as the Assam L of C was under his command, his GSI(b) staffs and FSOs would take such measures as they thought proper to secure it, and if people roamed about sensitive military areas, they did so at their own risk. This strong line eased the tension.

It was obvious that some method would have to be evolved to get these hush hush bodies up to the front line in reasonable secrecy, and without the possibility of their arrest by security personnel. The stumbling block was that the Heads of these services would not understand that forward of a certain point there were no ordinary transport services and that European civilians, or even any civilian, was immediately noticeable. They continued also to stress the secrecy angle. Finally after a meeting in a Calcutta hotel, it was agreed that we should be notified in a pre-arranged code of the arrival of any such agents, who would be travelling as civilians by ordinary train to Gauhati. There they would be met at an arranged rendezvous by an FS

NCO, taken to the FS House for the night, and then moved up to Manipur Road in secrecy by the Gauhati section. Summersell would then move them forward in his own transport.

A further problem emerged when the Americans started training personel in sabotage, prior to sending them into Burma; naturally without informing us. The upshot was that Railforce arrested some alleged saboteurs who were planting charges under railway bridges. It transpired that this was an American training exercise with, I am glad to say, dummy charges. On being told that the 'saboteurs' were lucky not to have been decapitated by the kukris of the Gurkhas, the American Officer in charge blithely answered that this might have encouraged later parties to be more careful.

We had a number of visitors to the Intelligence Detachment during the 1942–3 winter, of whom most had some connection with Intelligence. The incentive was that our guest room was more comfortable, the food in our small Mess better and the drink more plentiful than in the Reinforcement Camp. Further we had a certain amount of influence with Movement Control in the matter of reservations for rail journeys and the taxi service in Shillong.

One of our visitors was a very senior Indian Officer, Colonel 'Jix' Rudra, who was a member of the Commander in Chief's Josh (Morale) Group, Officers of the Josh Group, all Indian Colonels, visited Indian units to assess morale and had direct access to the Chief to discuss their findings. I had served with Jix in Landi Kotal when I was an acting Captain and he was a Major in the 4/15th Punjabis. He was a Christian whose father had been the Principal of St Stephen's College in Delhi. At the beginning of World War I, he was studying at Cambridge, but had enlisted in the Royal Fusiliers, fought in France and had been promoted to Sergeant. The end of the War found him awaiting a commission in the British Army, having completed an Officer Cadet course. However, the first Indians to hold combattant commissions in the Indian Army were being selected, and the India Office ordered him to report to Sandhurst to complete yet another Officer Cadet course. He objected to

this on the grounds that he was already qualified for a commission, and the authorities relented, but said that he must join
the final part of the course at Indore in India. This had the
effect of putting him in the second flight of those early
commissions, although his actual service counted from 1914.
Later on when the Indian Officers were tidied up into
'Indianised' Battalions, he was one of three exceptions, who
were so popular with the other Officers that strings were pulled
to retain them.

Jix was to tour the 4 Corps area and the L of C which
delighted me, particularly as I had a problem to discuss with
him. His tour programme had been drawn up in Delhi and was
completely divorced from reality. It presupposed that trains
would run to time instead of the more usual norm of three or
more hours late. I proposed, therefore, that he should have a
break in Gauhati, staying with us, to which higher authority
agreed.

My problem concerned the 1/11th Sikhs or the 1st King
George V's Own Battalion the 11th Sikh Regiment to give it
its full title. This unit had behaved very badly during the Burma
Retreat, so badly in fact that its disbandment was actually
considered. However to disband the senior and most prestigious
Battalion of this Regiment was not to be taken lightly and after
representations from the Maharaja of Patiala and other Sikh
Princes, it had been given another chance. After reorganisation
it was to come to Assam as Internal Security Battalion in the
Surma Valley. Sikhs must be worked hard if they are to be
kept from intrigue so the idea of this Battalion loafing about
in the Surma Valley filled me with alarm; I considered that
they should be sent to the front line to redeem themselves. I
brought this to Jix's notice, and as he told me years afterwards,
the Commander in Chief personally ordered the Battalion to
be sent to the Arakan front where its courage and behaviour
was exemplary. I can add that when I was at the Infantry
School during 1948–53, this unit was the best Demonstration
Battalion we had, and the oppostion included two Gurkha
units.

By the spring of 1943, matters had settled down to such an extent that a major reogranisation of the L of C was planned and this would certainly affect the future of the Intelligence Detachment.

CHAPTER FOUR

Headquarters — No 202 Line of Communications Area

T HE old set up, whereby HQ 4 Corps controlled the L of C, as well as commanding the fighting formations on the actual Burma front was, of necessity, a makeshift. It meant that a great deal of the time of the Commander and Staff was taken up with routine administrative matters, and, further, the HQ at Jorhat was too far back for effective control of the fighting troops.

The new set up meant that HQ 4 Corps moved forward to Imphal and a new HQ, formed from the old Assam L of C HQ, was to command all units in Assam in rear of the Corps. This formation was to be directly under Eastern Army and be named No 202 L of C Area. Under 202 would be three Sub Areas — at Dibrugarh, No 251, was to control the north eastern districts of the Assam Valley; an area which included the American staging airfields, the Digboi Oilfield and the Ledo Coal Mines. It would administer the elements of the Chinese Army, now arriving in north Assam after refitting in India, but command would rest with the American Army's China–India–Burma Command. At Shillong, No 252, was to control the western end of the Province. The H.Q. was positioned there to be equidistant from Gauhati and Silchar, although there were no troops stationed there, and, as a hill station, it was fast becoming a convalescent and leave centre for both British and American troops. How we at Gauhati envied them when the hot weather set in. No 253 controlled Manipur Road Base; although small in geographical area, it was the most important of the Sub Areas. The Field Security set up needed little adjustment; a section each at Dibrugarh, Silchar and Manipur Road Base, with small detachments at Shillong and Lumding.

No 202 Area HQ was to have a very much bigger staff than its predecessor. The General Staff Branch was to be headed by a GSO I with under him an Intelligence Section of five Officers headed by a GSO II, a GSO III for Operations and a GSO III (Camouflage), with a number of Camouflage Officers. The Gauhati Intelligence Detachment was to be absorbed, with myself as Chief Intelligence Officer (GSO II) and Peter Leefe and our IO as the I(b) subsection. A new GSO III and IO were to be posted in to form the I(a) subsection.

There was no way that I could avoid moving to Headquarters at the former Assam Government Survey School, because, as Chief Intelligence Officer, I had to be available when required by either the General or GSO I. This I did not take kindly to as the Survey School site was notoriously uncomfortable and lacking in amenities. I put up a case, however, that the I(b) subsection should remain where it was, as four miles out of the town, it would be too cut off from what was going on, and, further, it would be unable to carry out its more secret functions from a major military Headquarters; they should also retain the Station Wagon. I will admit to a certain amount of special pleading in the retention of the Gauhati house, as it would give me a comfortable place with electric light and fans to retreat to for a night or so when I felt like it.

The Survey School consisted of a number of wattle and daub hutments to which had been added a number of bamboo and reed huts called 'Bashas'. The General had one of the former as his combined office and living quarters and the others were used as offices and messes; the bashas were our living quarters. These had been built near a jheel or swampy lake, and when the monsoon came, the water rose so that my hut was on the edge instead of some twenty or so yards away. This caused an invasion of frogs and snakes in search of them. One evening I noticed one of the latter just inside the hut with a frog in its jaws — a blow with a stick at the point of junction and the frog hopped away in one direction and the snake slithered off in another. The proximity of the jheel with its high water table was a blessing as far as sanitation was concerned; all the Sappers had to do was to bore down to water level and then erect latrine buildings and seats over the holes. No emptying or other attention was needed.

The original hutments were wired for electric light; the current was produced by an antiquated DC dynamo, driven by an equally antiquated single cylinder paraffin engine. I had seen nothing like since my schooldays. It was a major operation to start it. First two lighted blow lamps were positioned on each side of the cylinder, then, when it was considered hot enough for the paraffin to have vapourised, the enormous flywheel was swung by hand; in due course it spluttered and finally started. Arrangements to wire up our living accommodation were in hand, but the existing machinery was not powerful enough to do more than light our Offices and Mess. A new modern generator only arrived a few weeks before my transfer.

'Phil' Rankin of the 2nd Royal Lancers was the General. He looked a typical cavalry Officer, sported a monacle and had a bald head which went crimson when he was annoyed. I had met him before when he was Brigade Major of the Sialkot Cavalry Brigade, and I, as a Second Lieutenant was doing my attachment to the 1st Dorsets. He did not remember an insignificant Subaltern, but I had cause to remember him as he said that my riding was not good enough for cavalry. I had thought this a bit hard as I had done an equitation Course with the 13/18th Hussars and owned my own horse. He denied all knowledge of me when I first reported to him, but when I reminded him of his remark that I could not ride, he said 'Well, can you now?'. I answered that I was a Handicap 1 at Polo. 'You won't get any here' he replied rather wistfully. He was a very efficient and considerate Commander, and I got on well with him, particularly later on, when for three months I was his principal Staff Officer, as GSO I. He had a great sense of humour, which stood him in good stead in a row with the 'Queen Bee' of the Womans Auxiliary Corps (India), the WAC(I)s. It had been ruled that no one should wear shorts after dusk as an anti malarial precaution; Phil considered that this very sensible rule should apply to the WAC(I)s also, and he issued orders that slacks instead of skirts must be worn. The Head WAC(I) sent a furious letter, in the course of which she wrote 'We women who have been a long time in the East are not bitten by mosquitos'. Phil not a whit abashed, wrote back 'I expect that your WAC(I)s are too fast for the mosquitos to catch them'.

My immediate boss, the GSO I, Lieutenant Colonel Jerrard of the Frontier Force Regiment had a somewhat Germanic countenance so he had been nicknamed 'Hindenberg' or 'Hindi' for short. He was considerably older than me, having served in World War I, but we got on well together and he allowed me a free hand in Intelligence matters. As the only GSO II in the Headquarters I was also his Deputy. I mention the disparity in age as by now, with the expansion of the Indian Army, Officers of my seniority were catching up on those who had been very senior to them and this sometimes caused friction. This was borne out in 202 Area when the senior Administrative Staff Officer, a Lieutenant Colonel, was from the same battalion as myself, and, in 1935, he had been a senior Major and I a Second Lieutenant. We had never got on in the battalion and now we were both Field Officers. The position became even worse later when I was acting GSO I. General Staff branch took precedence over the Administrative staff so, although, we were of equal rank, I had the higher status.

The two new additions, the I(a) sub section staff, were George Cockburn, the GSO III and Ian Bennett the Intelligence Officer. George was from the Burma Rifles, and had been an Officer of the Indian Civil Service in Burma. I was surprised that he had been allowed to join up, as with a very small cadre of civil Officers this was usually frowned upon. He was born in the same year as myself but was only finally appointed to the ICS in 1938. Ian Bennett of the Assam Regiment was rather older and was an educationalist who had come to India as tutor to the sons of the Maharaja of Darbhanga, a big landowner in Bihar. Both were University graduates, so intellectually superior to me, but neither had much experience; however they were two delightful people, who settled down quickly and ran a very efficient subsection. One irritation was our inability to find a good IO for Peter Leefe's sub section. Since the departure of 'Rama', no really good replacement had come our way. There was at this time a very great shortage of Officers trained in Security, and as Operational Intelligence was more popular, we got the 'left overs'. One such came to us direct from the Assam Oil Company. Higher Authority considered that a knowledge of Assam would make up for his lack of any Security training. He was a bumptious character who quickly got on the wrong side of Peter Leefe, and we were not sorry when he was removed to be the FSO of a new Field Security Section. This section was unique in that it consisted of an FSO and a Sergeant Major only, and was designed to work with the American-Chinese Forces in North Assam. The FSO had been chosen for his knowledge of the terrain, and the Sergeant Major, who had been in the Hongkong Police, for his knowledge of the Chinese. The FSO was a bad choice as his territorial knowledge did not compensate for the fact that he was both weak and untrained, and his subordinate was a 'wrong un'; between them they got us involved in several incidents with both the Americans and the Assam civil authorities, but this did not surface until the following year when I was Chief Security Officer of 14th Army.

Campbell, the GSO III (Camouflage), headed a motley crew of specialists, who were busily engaged in trying to persuade authority to do something about the airfields in Assam. He was highly efficient as was his team, but as they had been taken in direct from civil life their knowledge of the Army and its ways were scanty. One of his best Officers was a British subject from the Roumanian Oil Fields, whose family had been long domiciled there, and he himself had never left the country until he fled before the Nazi take over. He upset 'Hindi' Jerrard, bursting into his office, when ordered to go to Manipur Road, and declaring in a very gutteral accent 'I cannot go to the Manipur Roads'. On 'Hindi's' reply 'Why the devil not?', he came out with 'I haf but the von kidney and how to fight the high feeffers with but the von kidney'. Luckily Campbell arrived on the scene and pacified 'Hindi', subsequently sending the Roumanian elsewhere. He became one of the best of Campbell's team. The remainder of the Headquarters was made up of Administrative Staff Officers led by the Assistant Adjutant and Quartermaster General — my old Regimental colleague — Officers of the Royal Indian Army Service Corps, Indian Army Ordnance Corps, the Camp Commandant and finally the senior WAC(I) Officer for the area, about twenty Officers all told.

The War, meanwhile, had taken a dramatic turn for the better in the long term, but not on the Burma Front. In the Western Desert, 8th Army had captured Libya and were about to storm the Mareth Line and enter Tunisia, but the most important events for us were the American Naval victories in the Pacific. These drew off the Japanese surface vessels from the Bay of Bengal, and although passage was still hazardous by reason of submarine attacks, it was again possible to use the port of Chittagong to supply the troops in the Arakan, now part of 15 Corps. This Corps, largely as a result of prodding by Churchill, had made a feeble advance with the object of capturing Akyab. As they were nothing like ready to undertake such an operation, it was a failure, and when the inevitable Japanese counter attack came, all the ground gained was lost. There was still stalemate on the Manipur Front.

I had not been long in HQ 202 Area when we were put on 'Immediate Alert' as a result of a report of an alleged Japanese raid into North East Assam in the area of the Ledo Coalfields. While this seemed unlikely, it was possible that the Japanese could have infiltrated through the Hukawng Valley with the object of damaging the American airfields; somewhat like our later Chindit expeditions. The Alert was called off after a few hours as no trace of any Japanese could be found. The cause of the rumour emerged later.

The area of Fort Hertz on the northern most tip of Burma had remained in British hands with a garrison of the Burma Frontier Force. This was a thorn in the flesh of the Japanese, who mounted an operation to capture it. As it was not possible to reinforce the post, it was decided to evacuate the garrison. It was not considered feasible to do this by air, and to do so by land, over high mountain passes, when the party would contain women and children would be difficult. The well known naturalist, Kingdon Ward, who knew the area well, was consulted and he said that it could be done with the help of elephants. He was put in charge, and with the help of the Government of Assam, collected a large number of beasts with their mahouts. While moving by night in the Ledo-Margherita area, where Chinese Army units were encamped, the party stumbled into one of these camps. The Chinese opened fire killing two of the mahouts and killing or wounding several elephants; the remainder fled in all directions with or without their mahouts. This was bad enough, but the Chinese Commander sent a signal on a private wireless direct to the Generalissimo, General Chiang Kai-Shek, without the knowledge of his American superiors, stating that he had been attacked by Japanese. This report came back to Delhi, and onward to HQ Eastern Army, who had prudently ordered the Alert.

The problem now was—what was to be done about Fort Hertz? Even if the mahouts agreed to return, the re-assembling of the party would take time. By pure good fortune, the first Chindit expedition had just gone in and was creating havoc behind the Japanese lines. The Japanese column which was on its way to Fort Hertz turned back to deal with this menace and no further threat to the place occurred.

I was due for some leave and when the excitement had died down, I was granted three weeks in Calcutta. I had had the offer of the use of the flat of the MIO Calcutta, Major 'Roaring Rupert' Mayne, which would be much more comfortable than staying in a Hotel. Rupert Mayne was the nephew of the GOC in C, Southern Command, General Sir Mosely Mayne, and before the War had been employed in Calcutta with Caltex. Rupert had helped the Intelligence Bureau and the Calcutta Police, at the beginning of the War in identifying Axis business interests. He was later commissioned and appointed MIO Calcutta, still, of course, living with his wife in his pre-war flat. He was now taking a leave in the Hills so the flat was vacant.

I intended to use some of my time in Calcutta in getting in touch with HQ Eastern Army at Barrackpore and Calcutta Sub Area in Fort William. The GSO I(I) of Eastern Army. Lieutenant Colonel Boyes Cooper, was very appreciative of my work in Assam, and later on tried to further my career in Intelligence, but his well meaning efforts went wrong. I met the GSO II(Ib), Brian Whitehorn, who had been in business in South India before joining up. He was considerably older than I; in fact, although we had been at the same school, he had left before I arrived. My real host in Calcutta was Captain Maskell, the GSO III at Fort William, who showed me round and introduced me to the Police and other civil authorities. He was an Officer of the Intelligence Corps and was running a very efficient show in Calcutta. In view of what happened later, it was a good thing that I had made my number with him.

I had not long been back, when we were introduced for the first time to 'JIFs' i.e. personnel of the 'Japanese Inspired Forces', or as they were later called 'The Indian National Army' or INA. The Japanese, being very poor psychologists, would not believe that the majority of the Indian prisoners who joined them, did so more to gain better treatment than to fight actively against their former comrades. Thus, when they parachuted some such into India for espionage, they could not believe that these men had only volunteered to get home and would give themselves up as soon as they landed. The landing of three of these JIFs in Assam gave rise to the 'BATS' incident; BATS being the code name for these men. The three gave themselves up to the nearest military unit, and were sent down to Gauhati under escort. Eastern Army ordered us to send them as quickly as possible to Fort William, in secrecy, and on no account to inform the Civil Authorities or the Police of their arrival. Thus an FS escort was used instead of one from the Military Police. Calcutta Sub Area would send them on to Delhi for expert interrogation. Our escort was provided by the Sergeant Major and a Sergeant, together with two or three Indian ranks, from the Gauhati section.

The escort duly reported to me at HQ 202 for orders, and I took the opportunity to examine the prisoners' kit. One item was a 'tin' suitcase of a type much used by Indians. I opened it and saw that it had a built in wireless set, but before I could investigate further, 'Hindi' came in and said 'What are you playing at, Tony, they will miss the train, get them off at once'. So off they went. The two British NCOs I knew well, Starr, the Sergeant Major, had been a Corporal in the Gloucesters in Rangoon and was one of my first FS recruits. He was not particularly bright, but had a good stock of common sense and had done very well on the Retreat. The Sergeant was a bright young man, from the Royal Artillery, well educated, so I had asked his FSO for a special report on him with the idea of recommending him for a Commission.

During the journey to Calcutta this young man found Rs1000 in Rs10 notes hidden in the wireless. It so happened that they were forged, but he did not know this at the time. He suggested to Starr that they split the amount, but cheated him by giving him only Rs400 and keeping Rs600 for himself. After they had handed over their prisoners in Fort William, they had time on their hands, as the next train back was not until the following day. The Sergeant apparently had an account at Lloyds Bank so he paid his share in; the notes were good enough to pass the Teller at that time, and it was not until later that the forgeries were detected and the Bank sent for the Police, who asked the Military Police to arrest the pair.

It was at this stage that I was rung up by Maskell, who stated they were in military custody and would be claimed for trial by Court Martial, as was allowed by Indian Law. The trouble was that the CID were anxious to pursue their enquiries as to where the forgeries had come from, and to interrogate the men to further these enquiries. As the police had not been told about the 'BATS', I was fearful that a major Army-Police row might errupt, so I suggested to Maskell that he should contact the Calcutta Police Special Branch, with whom he had cordial relations, and explain that there were special circumstances regarding this forged money, and the easiest way out was to get the CID to drop the case and delete it from their records.

We would undertake to deal properly with the villains. This was done and the pair were brought back to Gauhati to face trial. It now transpired that the Sergeant was a real bad hat, who should never have been recommended for Field Security work. He was from a Public School, had gone to Cranwell before the war and been thrown out; after enlistment, he had been promoted to non commissioned rank several times and then had forfeited it for some misdemeanour. They were both convicted, reduced to the ranks, and sentenced to periods of detention, at the end of which they would have been returned to their parent units.

There was an amusing sequel. When Phil Rankin received the papers back from the Judge Advocate General's Department, they had noted that 'it is for consideration whether disciplinary action should not be taken against Major Mains for entrusting money to NCOs contrary to Kings Regulations'. Of course, I had an answer to this, which was that I had had no knowledge of the money, and Phil, highly amused, remarked 'Since when is forged money, money'.

A new problem was beginning to surface, and, again, one which would not have been the responsibility of Intelligence in other theatres. This was the morale of the civil population and the increasing number of incidents between them and the military forces. We became involved because of our close liaison with the Civil Authorities and the Police. The low morale resulted from the general slowing down of the administration, which was having its effect on the poorer sections of the community. British rule had protected the ordinary man from oppression and natural disasters. The basic principle of that rule, being that government and justice must be personal; the District Magistrate must be accessible to all the sundry, not only in his Court, but by spending much of his time touring his District. Unfortunately the old paternal rule was breaking down, and the very small cadre of Officers of the Indian Civil Service was stretched to the limit. All sorts of new burdens had been placed on them — rationing, and the requisitioning of land for the armed services to name but two. Leave was hard to get and for Europeans leave to Britain impossible, so the cadre had become stale and the old paternal rule neglected.

Eastern India was fast becoming a vast armed camp into which troops continued to pour. Besides British and Indian soldiers, who were a known quantity, and whose behaviour was usually exemplary, there were now Americans and Chinese whose behaviour was not always so good. The American troops, with the exception of the actual aircrew flying the dangerous 'hump' route into China, were Base and L of C troops, whose discipline was not always of the best. The main trouble was drink and women, the one usually leading to the other. Unfortunately the Government of Assam's Distillery was at Dikom close to the American airfields, and it produced the most frightful 'hooch' usually known as 'Dikom Death'. It was said that there was no difference between their whisky, gin and rum, except the colour, and Americans under the influence of this stuff might do anything. On several occasions American soldiers were beaten up by tea garden labourers who, often correctly, thought that they were after their women. Some events were not without their humor — one paragraph of the Inspector General of Police's monthly Report read 'an American soldier, who had had too much to drink, climbed onto the roof of the Dibrugarh-Tinsukia train, walked along the roofs until he reached the engine when he assaulted the driver; the train then stopped'.

About this time, I went on tour to Dibrugarh, again in a four wheeled saloon. The one that I was given, an old Assam Bengal vehicle, was somewhat decrepit and swayed so badly that I was nearly pitched out of bed. Nothing untoward occurred however, except that the engine of my train ran short of water and the fire had to be thrown out on the line, causing considerable delay. In Dibrugarh, I asked the District Superintendent of Police how his constables were coping with the Americans; up to now the only non Indians that they were used to were the British tea planters, who even after a party gave little trouble. He replied that it was simple — first, he impressed on his men that they were not Sahibs like the Planters, so they were not to be treated as such — second, should a single constable come across a drunken American causing trouble, on no account was he to tangle with him, but to go away and get reinforcements — third, when they had sufficient force they were to hit him with their lathis until he was insensible and finally to send for the American Military Police to remove him. When I asked him how the American authorities reacted; he said they were quite happy as this was the standard procedure used by their own Military Police.

Summer in the Survey Camp was not pleasant, hot and sticky, but I was able to get away to the I(b) House every now and then and spend a night with Peter Leefe. I was lucky, also, in that I could go on tour to Shillong to confer with the Police and even luckier, that the Sub Area Commander, Brigadier Gerry Crampton, had been my first Commanding Officer when I joined the 2/9th in 1935, and he would always give me a bed in Flagstaff House. On one visit I had to take with me a suspect who was wanted for interrogation. We had made elaborate arrangements with the Police to prevent any hold ups on the road, but on the return journey, not far from Gauhati, the car broke down. The suspect was travelling handcuffed on the back seat between two FS NCOs, and when we stopped for any reason he was pushed down between the seats and covered with a rug. We were considering what to do when a car drew up and out got an Indian gentleman, oozing goodwill, and offering us a lift in his car. Of course we said no and that another car would be coming for us, but he would not take that for an answer and wanted at least for me to go with him. It took quite a time to shake him off and all this time the wretched suspect was 'cooking' under the rug.

Sometime about the middle of June we heard that a major reorganisation was on the way. A new Command, South East Asia, was to be formed to take over, from India Command, all the forces land, sea and air, fighting the Japanese in South East Asia. This would be under the command of Admiral Lord Louis Mountbatten. To control the land forces, a Headquarters Allied Land Forces South East Asia was to be set up, in the first instance at Delhi. This meant that on the Burma front, the existing Eastern Army would be divided into 14th Army and Eastern Command. The former would command the forward troops and those on the L of C situated in Assam and the Chittagong Civil Division of Bengal; the remainder would be in Eastern Command. 14th Army HQ would be formed at Barrackpore alongside the old Eastern Army HQ, but would move to Comilla in eastern Bengal as soon as the reorganisation was complete and accommodation had been built. I learnt from Boyes Cooper that he would remain as GSO I(I) at Eastern Command as would Brian Whitehorn as GSO II(Ib), but this was not to happen for some time. Boyes Cooper also told me that he was recommending that I be transferred to the new HQ 14th Army as head of the security section (GSO II(Ib)), and as I would be the senior GSO II in the 'I' Branch, I would be Deputy to the GSO I, Tony Edwardes. However, before any of this happened, an event occurred which had exciting possibilities for me personally; 'Hindenberg' Jerrard was posted out to command a battalion, and his relief had not been notified to us. Thus as the senior, I took over as acting GSO I, while continuing in my original position. After three weeks had gone by, and no GSO I had appeared, I approached the General who told me to put up Lieutenant Colonel's badges of rank and to get the necessary orders published, and I had some hopes that I might get this appointment confirmed.

I had not long been in my new position when Transportation Branch asked my help in settling a matter with the Steamship Company and their somewhat cantankerous Agent. The Army had chartered somewhile back a few of the older steamers to carry troops and to allay the crews' fears, it was agreed that two AA Lewis Guns with Army gunners should be provided for each vessel. There were plenty of Lewis Guns in India but not AA mountings, so a considerable delay had occurred. Now when all was ready the Company started to make difficulties — if they were mounted on the bridge they would obstruct the Serang, particularily when he was berthing his vessel, and if they were mounted fore and aft, they would obstruct the view of the helmsman forward and the lookout aft, and so it went on. The relevant file showed that although the Army was to blame for the initial delay, a further delay of months rather weeks had been caused by the obstruction of the Steamer Company. As I said earlier the Agent was a very cantankerous Scot, who considered that the Army was a great nuisance to him and to his Company, and for this reason 'Hindi' had not forced the issue but had allowed matters to drift.

I felt that something had to be done so I rang up the Agent. He was unpleasant, even abusive — it was all the fault of the Army, they were a bunch of incompetents, had the matter been left in the hands of the Company all would have been settled long ago and so on. I endeavoured to pacify him by saying that I was genuinely trying to settle the matter, but that sent him off again, finishing up with 'The matter has been going on for four months now'; on this I lost my temper and retorted 'If it has been going on for four months, why the Devil are guns not mounted?' His reaction was to shout in broad Scots 'If ye canna speak properly to me ye can go to Hell', and banged down the phone.

I thought that I would give him a few minutes to cool off, and then try again. This time I took a high tone with him, saying that I was a Regular Officer of the Indian Army and that I was very proud of that Army. I went on to say that if I had blackguarded his Steamer Company in the way he had the Army, he would have been very angry, so why should I not be equally angry at his remarks. Further these measures were being taken to safeguard his crews and not just to annoy him. My calculated risk paid off and he became most reasonable and we quickly resolved the matter. A lot of his annoyance probably sprang from an incident in the previous summer, just after the Burma Retreat. A guarantee had been given to the labour at the Digboi Oil Field, that, should there be Japanese breakthrough into the Assam Valley, they would be evacuated in good time, and to that end a river steamer was stationed at Dibrugarh. It was to remain there until it was in danger of being hemmed in by low water. Unfortunately, owing to a lack of liason between the Army and the Company, it was not removed in time and immobilised for some months, and there was a long and bitter argument over compensation.

There was one more important task to carry out before I left Assam. We had received a Directive from HQ Eastern Army to liase with the Americans about the protection of the three or four 'hump' airfields in the north east part of the Province. This meant another trip to Dibrugarh to size up the problem. The troops allotted for close protection were a Battalion of the Royal Nepalese Army; this unit had detachments on each of the airfields. The six or so battalions which Nepal had sent to help us in the first winter of the War, had improved vastly in efficiency since then, but were still, with the odd exception, inferior to the Indian Army's Gurkha battalions. The first reserve was an Indian Territorial Battalion, again somewhat of an unknown quantity. Finally if more troops were required, then two Chinese Battalions would arrive from the Ledo area. There was no doubt that the operation would have to be very carefully controlled if success was to be achieved. The big fear was that each unit, as it arrived, would shoot up the previous one. This was a very real danger as far as the Chinese and Nepalese were concerned as both might be mistaken for Japs. A further complication was the presence of what the Americans described as 'combat teams'; they explained that these were an unspecified number of armed men in jeeps, who were really meant to combat parachutists, but were available at short notice to tackle any invader. The final answer was a joint Operation Order in the best Staff College style of each country. I signed 'for and on behalf of the General Officer commanding No 202 L of C Area', but the American Staff Officer went one better by signing 'for the Commander China-Burma-India Theater'. It was a good thing that the Plan never had to be tried out as I shudder to think of what might have been the outcome.

My time in Assam, had nearly run out as my posting to 14th Army had arrived, and a new GSO I was on his way. Phil Rankin did me a good turn by delaying both postings so that I was able to complete three months as a Lieutenant Colonel, which automatically made me a Temporary Lieutenant Colonel and a War Substantive Major: the significance of the latter rank was that now I could never go down below the rank of Major while the War lasted, although my substantive rank was still only that of Captain. In the reshuffle, George Cockburn was to take over from me and be upgraded, and Peter Leefe, also upgraded, was to go as GSO II(Ib) to HQ ALFSEA. At first I wondered why Peter had been selected to go to a Headquarters above mine, but I subsequently learned that Boyes Cooper had thought that this would be a better arrangement and of more advantage to myself. Although Peter would be in a superior Headquarters, he would not be the section Head as there would be a GSO I(Ib) under a Brigadier (I) as Chief Intelligence Officer. I would not only be the section Head, but also, Deputy to the Chief Intelligence Officer, and this might well lead to higher things; unfortunately it did not work out quite like that. So at the end of September, I said my farewells and took the train to Calcutta to start a further phase of my career in Intelligence.

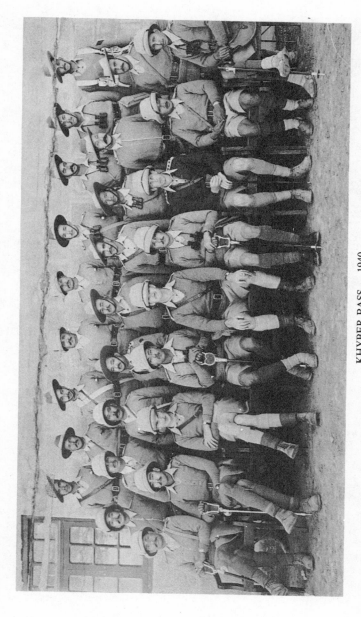

KHYBER PASS — 1940.
Frontier Warfare Course for Officers of the Royal Nepalese Army.
Author — third from left.

IRAQ — 1941.
Officers of the Intelligence Branch lunching with a local Sheikh.
Author — left, front row.

OFFICE OF THE INSPECTOR GENERAL OF POLICE, ASSAM.

SECRET

D.O.No. 4471-C

Shillong,
The 2nd October 1943.

My dear Mains,

      Very many thanks for your D.O.No.565/1/GS(I)(b) of the 27th September 1943 which I very much appreciate.

      May I reciprocate and say how very useful your co-operation has always been during the past year when so much has happened in and around Assam.

      With all good wishes for the future.

Yours sincerely,

H.C.R.Cumming.

Major A.A. Mains.
Head quarters, Eastern Army,
C/o.No.12 Advance Base, P.O.
    INDIA.

DY: GENERAL MANAGER'S OFFICE,
B. & A. Railway,
GAUHATI, the 4th October,1943.
17th

D.O.No. 23/See.

My dear Col.Mains,

      Many thanks for your letter and your kind remarks about my help and co-operation.

    2. I have only to compare the awful time we were having last year to the present peaceful days to appreciate the hard work you must have put in to give us the required security. I am indeed very thankful to you and to all your officers and men for this.

    3. I wish you best of luck in your new sphere of activities.

Yours sincerely,

Q.Z. Hussain

Lt.Col.A.A.Mains,
H.Q., Eastern Army,
C/O No.12 Advance Base P.O.
India.

ASSAM — 1943.
Letters of appreciation from the Assam Police and Railway Authorities.

ASSAM — 1942–3.
Author's Security Warrant Card.
Authorising him to be in any place at any time and any dress.

WANA — 1945.
Boxing Day Meet of the Wana Hounds.
Brigade Headquarter's Mess.

AGRA — 1946.
GENERAL STAFF BRANCH — HQ CENTRAL COMMAND.
Front row from left — 4th Author — 6th Brig Barker
7th General Scoones — 10th Major Addison.
2nd row — 5th from left Major Moorshead.

AGRA — 1946.
Author driving to Office

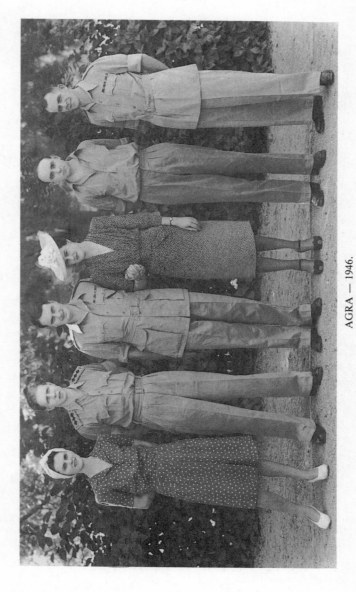

AGRA — 1946.
Wedding Group

Left to right — Mrs Moorshead — Captain Hurst — Major & Mrs Mains
Hubert Evans ICS, District Magistrate — Major Moorshead.

1948.
The Author.

CHAPTER FIVE

Headquarters, 14th Army

T HE world situation was very much better when I left Assam than it had been when I arrived. The Russians had repulsed the Germans, captured Stalingrad and relieved Leningrad; Allied Forces had occupied Sicily and had a toehold on the mainland of Italy, and the Americans had command of the sea in the Pacific and were edging forward island by island.

The Burma Front was still stagnant, as there was little activity on the Manipur border and in the Arakan local advances were met by Japanese counter attacks. The most important event was the operation later to be known as 'Chindit I'. This was the brainchild of Brigadier Orde Wingate, who managed to get Wavell on his side for what was an extremely unorthodox operation. It involved the intrusion, into Burma behind the Japanese lines, of a weak Brigade Group of one British and one Gurkha battalion with a Commando Company. Nothing concrete was achieved, except perhaps the stopping of the Japanese advance on Fort Hertz, mentioned in the previous Chapter. Indeed Wingate's detractors later said that he was the only man who had completely written off a Gurkha battalion. It did prove, however, that such an operation was feasible and paved the way for the larger operation in 1944.

14th Army HQ was being formed in Barrackpore, by the simple expedient of splitting HQ Eastern Army into two. The actual venue was Government House, the one time country residence of the Viceroy and later of the Governor of Bengal, overflowing into the bungalows of the surrounding Cantonement. I was allotted a place in No 1 Mess, a bungalow on the banks of the River Hoogly, with the bedrooms in hutments in the grounds. My Gurkha servant who had replaced Faudebahadur, Birman Sunwar, greatly approved of being in civilisation again. I also acquired a mongoose, or rather it acquired me, coming every morning to share a banana when I was having my morning tea.

The three or four weeks that we spent in Barrackpore, before the move to Comilla were mainly taken up with splitting the files with Brian Whitehorn, who was remaining with Eastern Command. I cannot remember if operational control had passed to 14th Army at this time, but whether it had or not would have made little difference as many of the new staff had occupied similar posts in Eastern Army. The GOC in C, Bill Slim, was new, but not the BGS. The GSO I(I), Tony Edwardes was the old GSO II(Ia), and had brought practically the whole of the Operational Intelligence staff with him. My security section was mostly new, except that the GSO III, 'Jimmy' James a Gunner, was from the old Command.

These weeks were almost like leave for me. Calcutta was only 30 minutes away by suburban train and one could get in any day after work. I did this, once or twice, staying with Rupert and Cicily Mayne, and returning on the following morning. We were allowed also one afternoon off a week, and this provoked an incident which was going to cause me some trouble in the future. Tony Edwardes insisted that, as his Deputy, I should stand in for him if he was absent, although I had no knowledge as yet, of the operational scene. Thus on several occasions, when the BGS sent for me to produce some piece of operational intelligence, I had to get the GSO II(Ia) to answer his queries. The BGS was not pleased nor was Tony on his return, and it made me look a fool. This underlined the basic fact that Ia and Ib Officers were not interchangeable, but it took a very long time for this to sink into the minds of those who decided upon Intelligence postings.

We set off for Comilla in a number of special trains, rail to Goalundo on the Padma River, then steamer to Chandpur and rail again to our destination. I had travelled this route the year before when I had to return to Assam this way owing to the breaches on the northern line. I was to travel it again a number of times on my visits to Calcutta, and I always enjoyed the peaceful sail of about six hours duration. While train travel in eastern India was usually overcrowded, dirty and slow, the steamers were always in immaculate condition, with clean comfortable berths, and excellent food and drink. We had an amusing incident on the final leg of the journey. I had warned my fellow travellers to close the wooden shutters and bolt the doors of their train compartments because of thieves, but a number, new to India, laughed at me and said nothing would induce them to comply on a hot Indian night. The next morning there was a great commotion, as several Officers had had their clothes stolen and were forced to borrow or else detrain in their pyjamas.

Comilla was the Headquarters of the Tippera Civil District, situated on the main railway line from Chittagong to Assam. Close by was the native State of Tripura, and its capital Agartala. In actual fact there was originally just the one State of Tripura, but the British had annexed half of it, so the British District was spelled Tippera to distinguish it from the State. There was a small colony of Europeans and Armenians living there in peace time, engaged in the jute trade. The District had a bad reputation for political terrorism, and a British Superintendent of Police had been murdered in the thirties.

HQ 14th Army was located in the District Kutchery, that is the District Magistrate's Offices and Courts; a new makeshift Kutchery had been built for him in a small town fifteen miles away. The clerical staff were housed in the jail, with openings cut in its outer wall. The most notable feature of the town was a large 'Tank' or artificial pond around which were situated the houses of the 'Jute wallas'; these had been requisitioned for Officers Messes, and as in Barrackpore, the Mess was in the building and the living quarters hutments on the bank of the Tank. I was interested in the temporary barracks provided for HQ's garrison battalion, the 25th Gurkhas. They had been built originally for the 1st Battalion of my Regiment, who had been drafted into the District in the early thirties for anti terrorist duties. The somewhat flimsy wooden hutments on stilts

— 87 —

had been the subject of a number of stories told to me when I joined. The first expert who saw them predicted that they would fall down immediately one of the hurricanes, which periodically swept up the Bay of Bengal, arrived; so heavy wooden buttresses were fixed to the walls. The next expert said — no, they would be uprooted, so heavy steel cables were passed over the roofs and fixed to concrete holdfasts. I thought these were tall stories but truth is stranger than fiction, there were the barracks with the buttresses and cables still in position.

I was now to enter what proved to be the least pleasant part of my time in Intelligence. There were two reasons for this — the first was that the old pioneering period was over and I was rapidly becoming merely a Staff Officer keeping files, attending conferences and producing reports rather than getting out and about visiting the FS Sections — the second was that try as I might, I just could not get on with my GSO I.

The Field Security had now reached its full strength, in the 14th Army area of about 24 Sections. These comprised a section for each Division and L of C Sub Area, together with sections for L of C Area, Corps and Army HQs. There were also two specialised sections, one for Chittagong Port and one, No 615, for the American-Chinese Forces. Everything was now routine so I settled down to the office work of reading and collating the Security Summaries of lower Formations and the FS Sections, together with the Censorship reports and, of course, those from the Police. These were evaluated and finally collated into a Monthly Army Security Summary. There was no place for touring, and it was not encouraged. I only made three tours in the whole year to visit Ib staffs and FS sections and one of these was abortive.

I had some difficulties with Karachi, notably with Lieutenant Colonel Joe de Vine, the Commandant of the Indian Intelligence Corps and Chief Instructor of the FS Wing. Joe, who had been appointed when 4 Corps refused to release me for this post, was a one time Officer of the Burma Police, who after retirement, had joined up, like Peter Leefe, in the early days of the War and had served in one of the original FSP Sections in France. He had come to India straight from the UK and had no experience of the work of Sections in the East. He ordered the sections in 14th Army to submit copies of their monthly reports to him; in spite of the word 'ordered', I had no objection as I considered that these reports would be of value for training new sections. He then started to take objection to what the sections were doing and once again tried to 'order' them about. I had to point out to him that beyond keeping sections up to strength his responsibility ceased when they left Karachi. Operational control was exercised by the formation to which a section had been allotted, subject to the any overall control by the Ib staff of higher formation.

The difficulties that I had with Joe de Vine were minor compared with my relations with my GSO I. The trouble was a clash of personalities; Tony was technically an Officer of the Indian Army, The Royal Indian Army Service Corps, but he was really from British Infantry. He had sent in his papers before the War and on being recalled had managed to get attached to the Indian Army. There was no doubting his energy and efficiency, but he was a cold calculating person, who did not mix with those he considered his subordinates. His attitude was that of the senior subaltern of a British battalion at the time when such had 14 or 15 years service. I was accustomed to the much easier relationship of an Indian Army unit, where a Major and a 2/Lieutenant were often doing the same job, so it was obvious that he and I would never get on together. His previous appointment had been the Head of the I(a) section so he kept a very tight hold on it, and would not let the section head, the GSO II(Ia), run his own show. This meant that this section was in a state of incipient mutiny, with frequent requests for a return to Regimental duty from its members. A lot of the trouble was caused by the absolute lack of any amenities or recreational facilities in Comilla, which caused many of the staff to become stale. Every day, including Sunday, was the same so I tried to introduce some variety by giving each of my Officers an afternoon off a week unless there was something important on, when they had to return to the office for an hour or so after tea.

I was more fortunate because, besides three tours, I was able to get away to Calcutta once a month for a security conference with the Police, and once I was called up to HQ ALFSEA in Delhi to discuss the security situation. The first of my tours was completely abortive; with some difficulty, I had persuaded Tony to agree to my visiting HQ 15 Corps in the Arakan, a trip which could only be undertaken by road. I had only got a short distance south of Chittagong, when the winter rains started and all traffic was prohibited on the dirt road, so I was marooned for some three days, until I got Army HQ to instruct Corps HQ to allow me to return.

My second tour was back to Assam. I had got George Cockburn to assemble all the GSO IIIs of Sub Areas and the FSOs for a conference. This was a great success, and in particular, it enabled me to deal with the problem of No 615 Section. I had received a number of reports from George, mainly passing on complaints from the civil authorities on the behaviour of the two members of this section. It appeared that the FSO and the Sergeant Major were hand in glove with the Americans against the local Political Agent. The trouble seemed to have arisen because the Americans thought the PA was being unco-operative, when all he was trying to do was to cushion the impact of the American-Chinese forces on the life style of his tribals. The whole matter was comparatively trivial, but owing to the stupid behaviour of the two members of the section had blown up out of all proportion. I had tried to deal with the situation by posting away the FSO for training and posting in the best Officer that I had available.

During the course of the conference the new FSO came to me and complained that he was getting nowhere — the Americans would not co-operate and the Sergeant Major was almost openly hostile. We were lucky that we had an American Intelligence Liaison Officer present, so I marched him and the FSO straight up to the General, Phil Rankin. The pair of them told their respective stories. The General got redder and redder in the face, a sure sign that he was annoyed, when it transpired that the Americans had made no attempt to contact him. He then castigated that American Officer, telling him in no uncertain terms that any trouble of this nature must be brought to his notice, so he could take it up with the Government of Assam, and not be dealt with in a hole and corner fashion.

My final tour was to Chittagong and was largely as a result of a moan from the FSO of the Port Section. They had been given a house on the waterfront close to a jetty. This Jetty was used for loading barges and it so happened that what was being loaded was rotten bully beef. This corned beef was part of a consignment bought by the British Government for emergency rations should Britain have been invaded. When the threat receded, the beef was sent to the Middle East for the same reason, and subsequently had gone half round the world before it had been unloaded at Chittagong, as the Captain of the ship, which had it in its hold had flatly refused to take it any further. It had been landed on the Jetty for loading into barges which were to be towed out to sea for dumping. When I arrived the stench was overpowering and the FSO said that it had been like this for some weeks and little attempt was being made to speed things up. As far as I could see only two coolies were working — well, if throwing a tin every now and then into a lighter, could be called working. I contacted the Administrative Commandant who promised to speed matters up. There were a number of ships in Port and the FSO took me on board one for drinks with the Captain; a welcome change from Indian gin and rum.

My trip to Delhi was somewhat hair raising. I had been given a Priority place on the through Comilla-Delhi RAF Transport run. The plane was a demilitarised Hudson, which left Comilla in the late afternoon for the short hop to Calcutta, and continued onwards, with one refuelling stop at Cawnpore, the next morning. This flight took place during the monsoon season, and therefore I was prepared for a bumpy ride. We had a fair run into Calcutta but the next morning, the clouds were as black as ink. I should mention here that there were neither seats nor seat belts, you had to make yourself as comfortable as possible on your bedroll. We all hoped that the flight would be postponed and that the two or three passengers would be sent on by train, but, not so. We took off and the pilot tried to find a way past the dense clouds to the west, by going round by the north, but unsuccessfully, so he got a message to the AA Command that he was going out south across the defended zone, and would they please refrain from firing at us. We got out eventually, but were an hour and a half late at Cawnpore, feeling very sick and much in need of a lavatory, as there was none on the plane. A pleasant two hour flight followed and I was met at Delhi to my great joy by Peter Leefe.

The official reason for my visit was to discuss the security arrangements for the hoped for capture of Akyab, and I was to take back with me a number of documents. These were lists of Japanese supporters, who were to be arrested immediately, and lists of those who would be needed to get some sort of administration going. In actual fact, they were not used, at any rate at that time, as on the day that I arrived back, the Japanese attacked and surrounded our forces in the Arakan. I had another and more personal reason, and that was to get Peter Leefe to help me to obtain a battledress. I had lost all my warm uniform on the Burma Retreat and was unable to get any in Eastern India as sales were restricted, on the grounds that the climate was not cold enough to warrant issues of a uniform in very short supply. This meant that I had to wear khaki drill bush shirts in a bitterly cold Delhi, as I did not even have a khaki drill jacket, these having been lost in Burma too. I managed to get my battledress by Peter maintaining that it was for him.

The monthly visits to Calcutta were a great joy and break from the routine of Headquarters. A retired Inspector General of Police, Sir Douglas Gordon, had been appointed Civil Security Adviser to 14th Army and Eastern Command, and he had instituted a monthly conference of the Deputy Inspector Generals of Police (CID) of Bengal, Assam, Bihar and Orissa, the Head of the Special Branch of the Calcutta Police with the GSOs II(Ib) of 14th Army and Eastern Command. Sir Douglas was a charming man, whom I came to respect and like; this must have been mutual as he invited me to stay with him and Lady Gordon on my visits. In addition to attending the conference, I took the 14th Army Security Summary to be printed at the Government of Bengal's Security Press; and then brought back the finished product with me on my return. At first I went both ways by air in the ramshakle Dakota laid on by the RAF for the daily mail run, but they took exception to the weight of the printed Summaries, and to my great delight I made the return trip by rail and steamer.

A resumé of the current military and political situation on the Burma front may be of interest. The Three Power Conference in Teheran had given ALFSEA two tasks; one was the capture of Akyab, and the other the mounting of another 'Chindit' operation. Stilwell had been called to the Conference and had produced a very complicated, and to some extent, unworkable plan. There were three main elements. First, the flying in of a large force to land behind the Japanese lines in Burma. This force at first known as Special Force, and later given the cover name of 3rd Indian Division, was to consist of, with the exception of four Gurkha battalions, British and West African troops only. Wingate considered Indian troops useless and in this he was backed up by Churchill. The actual composition was three all British Brigades, one West African Brigade and two alleged Indian Brigades of part British and part Gurkha soldiers. The second element was the intrusion into Burma, via the Hukawng Valley of the Chinese troops under American Command, and finally an attack on north Burma by the Chinese Yunnan Reserve Army.

Bill Slim was extremely sceptical of the success of the plan; having witnessed the destruction of the 'Chindit I' troops for little material gain. Further, having commanded BurCorps in the Retreat, he had little faith in the ability of the Chinese to fit into a co-ordinated plan. There was also a political objection — the Kachins of north Burma were strongly pro British and anti Chinese as China had long coveted their lands. Bill Slim was adamant that any long range penetration must be done in such a way that a link up with 14th Army was possible, and the Yunnan project must be abandoned. He got his way.

In late February and early March everything happened at once. The Japanese attacked in the Arakan and managed to penetrate the front line and surround and attack the HQ and administrative area of 7th Indian Division. Had this happened a year or so earlier, the Division might well have withdrawn, leaving the way open for the Japanese to destroy the whole of 15 Corps. Now things were different, British and Indian troops were no longer frightened nor deterred by Japanese outflanking movements, and when outflanked by the enemy, merely formed defensive 'Boxes', which were supplied by the air, and waited for the Japanese attack to peter out. The Arakan offensive was intended to draw off British forces from the Manipur front, which was next attacked. This was extremely serious as the Japanese not only surrounded 4 Corps in the Manipur plain but penetrated into the Naga Hills at Kohima, only a short distance from the railway at Manipur Road Base. The main body of 4 Corps, supplied from the air, stayed put, and the spirited defence of Kohima, finally put paid to any idea of a shattering Japanese victory.

There is no doubt that the hidebound attitude of the Japanese actively contributed to their defeat. This was borne out by events at Kohima. The Japanese plan was to capture Kohima come what may, but when it became obvious that they would be unable to do this, the logical move would have been to bypass it and move to cut the railway. Had this been done, even by a small raiding party, all the labour — be it tea garden, oilfield or coal mines in north Assam would have run. This situation was a great worry to 202 Area. General Phil Rankin decided that, as a precaution, the wives and families of the Planters on the small number of tea gardens astride the railway line north of Manipur Road should be evacuated. This was done in a great hurry, and the evacuees arrived in Calcutta after a very uncomfortable journey, with only the clothes they stood up in. A furious complaint was made to HQ 14th Army by the Indian Tea Association about the high handedness of the Army. It was extremely unfortunate that this quarrel should have arisen as the Army had the highest regard for the work of the Planters, many of whom had been refused permission to join up as it was considered that the export of tea to Britain was vital to the war effort, and further all the airfields, pipe lines, road improvements and so on had been constructed by tea garden labour, working under the supervision of the tea garden staff and co-ordinated by the ITA.

Meanwhile the Chindit expedition had got under way and we were involved in trying to oversee security for the operation. This was very difficult as the US Airforce personnel, who were to fly them in, had no idea of security and careless talk was rife. We were also involved in the security of the airfields at which the victorious Chindits landed on their return. They were in such poor physical shape from the hardships which they had endured that it was considered unwise for their condition to become generally known at the time.

It was about this time that Higher Authority decided to demarcate the line between Security (GSIb) and Deception (GSId). They decreed that any moves to provoke a reaction by the enemy was deemed to be Deception, but action to prevent the enemy from knowing what we were doing was to be Security. Both had been done up to now, in the main, by GSI(d).

Our new technique was soon to be tested. It was intended to move the 11th East African Division from Ceylon to Chittagong during the summer. The shortage of shipping meant that it would have to be done in two or more echelons spread over several weeks, and while the Japanese no longer had command of the Bay of Bengal, it was known that submarines were operating. The danger was that Japanese intelligence sources might discover the presence of part of 11th EA Division at Chittagong, while some elements were still in Ceylon, and putting two and two together, would lie in wait for the later convoys. We were lucky that we had the 81st and 82nd West African Divisions in the Arakan, and we very much doubted if any enemy agent would know the ethnic difference between West and East Africans. The first part of the plan was to use this advantage. All the East African units were given temporary West African names, particular attention being given to advance parties. The next problem was mail; this we solved partly by putting a two weeks delay on all mail going out from units still in Ceylon and partly by sending all mail from those already in Chittagong back to Ceylon to be postmarked and rebagged by the Field Post Office there.

The situation on the civilian front was very bad. The Bengal famine had taken its toll and the number of Army-Civilian incidents had greatly increased. There was no doubt that the average villager or lowly town dweller had lost all faith in the ability of British rule to defend his interests. The Bengal famine is alleged to have claimed a million lives, and was a completely man made disaster. There was undoubtably a shortage of rice due to the loss of Burma, India's traditional supplier, and the great difficulty, in war time, of finding an alternative supply or the shipping to move it. The actual deficit, however, was not great and all other Provinces managed to avoid disaster by strong administrative action. Bengal was ruled by an inefficient and corrupt Moslem League Ministry, which the acting Governor was reluctant to depose. In addition there had been a change of Viceroy and Wavell, the new incumbent, had hardly had time to assess the position. Strong administrative action was required to get such rice as there was on to the market, particularly in the villages as it was considered quite impossible to introduce rationing in rural areas; it was difficult enough to enforce it in the towns. The Ministry allowed matters to drift, and even hindered the efforts of officials to deal with the situation, which resulted in an influx of starving poor into the towns and, in particular, into Calcutta. The famine only touched the landless labourers in the villages and the urban poor. The farmers not only had plenty of rice for themselves and their families, but were hoarding it to sell at inflated prices to the well to do in the towns. The British soldier was completely bewildered when asked to contribute money to a famine relief fund; he could not understand how it was possible to buy food if, allegedly, there was none. Many units fed the local poor with left overs from their cookhouses. However the Viceroy took energetic action and got the Bengal Ministry dismissed and provided a new strong man as Governor, the Australian, Casey. Strong action followed, Casey revitalised the Bengal administration, and forced the new Ministry to set up camps in rural areas into which the starving poor from the towns were moved. The Viceroy did not trust the civil officers so he set up a corps of Army Officers, who knew the country well, to oversee these measures. 'Roaring Rupert' Mayne was one of those selected.

The Army made a great effort to avoid taking more off the country than was strictly necessary, and a Directorate of Local Resources was set up in 14th Army. All static units, such as Heavy AA and Depots, were encouraged to lay out vegetable gardens and keep poultry. Some one had the bright idea of setting up a brewery at Comilla and an analysis of the local water was taken to see, if by the addition of certain chemicals, it would approximate to that at Burton on Trent, however the idea faded out. The Local Resources Branch got us into trouble with the Special Branch of the Calcutta Police. They had bought for breeding a number of ducks in Chungking and persuaded the Americans to fly them to Calcutta for distribution to static units, but they neglected to inform us, who would have asked 'I' Branch at Fort William to deal with any problems connected with their arrival. The importation of the ducks might well have caused difficulties with the Customs, but worse still they imported without any authority a number of Chinese 'duck handlers'. Their arrival at Dum Dum Airport, unannounced, without passports, and unable to speak a word of any language other than Chinese, left the Police decidedly unamused.

The number of incidents involving troops and the civil population began to cause considerable concern. We had now in addition to the Americans, West and East Africans. The former affected to despise the Bengalis, and were not all that well disciplined but the East African Division, on the other hand, gave little trouble. The worst offenders, by far, were the black American troops, with the white Americans only marginally better. The West Africans record was not good possibly because of their attitude to the local population, but as has been said the East Africans record was much better. At the bottom of this league table were the British and Indian troops and the RAF. The Americans obviously considered that they could ill treat the local population with impunity, cases of rape were numerous, and of murder also. In one incident an American shot dead a Sikh soldier in an altercation over a traffic accident, and this could have led to a very serious fracas, had it not been for the discipline of the Sikh NCO present. He calmed his men and said that they were not to touch the American, but they would take him to their Sahib, who would know what to do. The murder of a Sikh taxi driver in Calcutta necessitated the American Base Commander and his Officers walking in the funeral procession. Later the US China-Burma-India Command took energetic steps to restore discipline.

We had mastered the threat of sabotage on the Assam Railways, but the capacity was still very low. The Indian railwayman's heart was not in his job, but he was not entirely to blame; prices of basic foodstuffs had risen far above what he could afford, and he and his family were in real distress. The Anglo Indian staff were partly militarised, as they were members of the local railway unit of the Auxiliary Force, and an attempt was made to raise the status and ameliorate the lot of the Indian railwayman by forming 'Defence of India' units and inviting them to enlist. The main incentive was free and sufficient rations, but the men had to accept military discipline of a sort, and could be punished if they left their posts. The scheme was not entirely a success. A Stationmaster as a responsible civilian railway employee could usually hold his own with senior Army Officers but was at a disadvantage when uniformed as a Second Lieutenant. The menial staff looked anything but soldierly in dirty uniforms, often with their shirts outside their shorts, as they would normally wear them, but with 'D of I' shoulder titles proclaiming to be soldiers. A new plan was next put forward; this was to hand over to the US Army transportation troops the operation of the metre gauge line from Parbatipur Junction to Dibrugarh, including the Pandu-Amingaon ferry. The railway staff would remain, and the Stationmasters would continue to deal with passengers and the commercial side, but the Americans would drive and provide the Guards for all troop and military goods trains. More important still was the posting of an American traffic overseer to each station to keep the Assistant Stationmasters on their toes and to see that there was no hold up of traffic.

The plan was by no means universally well received, and this was not surprising in view of the American attitude to the civilian population. I attended a high level conference in Calcutta to discuss how the Indian staff would react. We were expecting fireworks from the General Manager of the Bengal and Assam Railway, Cuffe. He was an extremely efficient railwayman who knew the area well as he had been the head of the small metre gauge privately owned Assam Bengal line, now a part of the B & A system, before being elevated to run the large and prestigious state owned Bombay Baroda and Central India Railway. He had the reputation of not suffering fools gladly and his return to eastern India had put the fear of god into many of his subordinates. He turned the scale in favour of the scheme, by saying that he thought the injection of an American, prepared to work flat out to keep traffic moving, would boost the morale of his Indian staff. There was no doubt that the plan was a great success, but unfortunately there was some anti American propaganda, which took the form of implying that the line was being operated in a reckless way, leading to many accidents. It was unfortunate that a lot of wreckage from the sabotage derailments of the previous year was still to be seen beside the line, and this was often falsely attributed to the Americans.

The encirclement of 4 Corps had caused us some anxiety as the Japanese infiltrated into the mountains between Manipur State and southern Assam, and between the Chin Hills and eastern Bengal. In the tribal areas of these Provinces, 'V' Force was well established and could be relied on to provide timely warning of any Japanese raiding parties, but there was one area not covered, this was the Native State of Tripura. The greater part of the State was mountainous tribal territory between the Lushai Hills District of Assam and the Chittagong Hill tracts of Bengal. It was not considered desirable for political reasons for 'V' Force to operate in the State without the Maharaja's permission, which so far had not been forthcoming. To make matters worse, the misgovernment and oppression of the tribal people by the State Government had occasioned sporadic rebellion, a fertile field for enemy infiltrators.

Tripura was not considered either large enough or important enough to warrant a British Resident, but was part of the Eastern States Agency operating from Calcutta. The Civil Security Adviser, on behalf of 14th Army, had represented strongly that a Resident, or at least, a Political Agent should be appointed in view of the strategic importance of the area. The Government of India refused our request but agreed to post a junior Officer of the Political Department as a Political Liason Officer. This Officer did not get very far in his dealings with the Maharaja's Government, and advised that it would be better if Sir Douglas requested an official interview with His Highness. This request was granted and I was detailed to accompany him to Agartala, the State capital. As this place was only a few miles from Comilla, one would have thought that the whole matter could have been dealt with in a day, but not so, it took three days and ended with a somewhat bizarre incident.

We arrived at the Palace only to be met by the Political Liason Officer with the news that HH could not see us that day, but we were welcome to stay in the State Guest House. In actual fact we did not get our audience until the third day, but in the meantime we were very comfortable in the Guest House, an annexe of the Palace, lavishly furnished by Maples. There was plenty to eat and drink and the Head Cook was ordered to report to us daily to discuss each day's Menu. Our meeting with HH and his brother, the Home Minister, when at last it did take place, was somewhat inconclusive, but the situation was ceasing to be either of importance or urgency. The Japanese had been decisively defeated at Kohima and were pulling back into Burma, so the possibility of infiltrators was becoming remote. At the end of our meeting, His Highness turned to Sir Douglas and said 'Sir Douglas, we must have a party', and to one of his underlings 'Go-Go-Go-Go to those Hospitals; go to those Matrons, those Sisters, invite them to the Palace to dinner tonight'. He was referring to the two or three British Military Hospitals established in or around Agartala.

In due course we assembled in the main hall of the Palace, where Calcutta rum was lavishly served. HH moved among the guests followed by his Gurkha orderly who carried HH's drinking vessel, a silver cup with a lid; the State Army had a Gurkha unit, the 3rd Tripura Rifles. After a while I was summoned and His Highness suggested that, as his State was almost in the front line and his troops were under command of 14th Army, he should wear the 14th Army 'Flash' on his uniform. I agreed with him but pointed out that he was already wearing the flashes of his own forces. However using a little diplomacy, I indicated that Sir Douglas, as Adviser to both 14th Army and Eastern Command, wore both formation's flashes, one on each shoulder, so why should he not do the same. The idea appealed to him, but could a 14th Army flash to complement that of the Tripura Forces be found. Immediately I whipped of one of mine, a safety pin was quickly found and the flash affixed to the Maharaja's shoulder — could the Political Department have done better?

A four course European style dinner followed with more rum, and on conclusion HH led the company down to a courtyard at the rear of the Palace. Like many Indian Palaces which were very grand in the front, this one tailed off to a collection of stables and sheds, housing the menial servants, the Guard and the sacred cow. At the bottom of the stairs was a wretched panther cub in a very small cage, being tormented at intervals by the Guard. One of the Matrons, a lady of strong views, told HH that this wretched animal should be shot rather than be kept in such conditions. HH who was in that pleasant condition known as 'drink taken', replied 'Certainly, dear Lady, shoot it, shoot it'. Whatever my personal feelings might have been regarding the animal, I had a job to do, and it was no part of my job to condone anything which might upset our relations with the Maharaja. I could see, that, although he had told the Matron to shoot the cub, he might think very differently about it in the morning. I, therefore, started to get the company moving back up to the Palace, and I thought all was well, when the Matron, who had started to ascend the stairs, turned round, took a Sten gun from one of the Guard and shot the animal. Luckily by morning, HH had forgotten the incident and we heard no more.

While I was at Comilla, I got involved in what is now a Military Police responsibility, 'close protection' of VIPs. I had tried to persuade General Quinan in Iraq to let me send an FS NCO with him, when he was taking his evening walk along the banks of the Tigris at Bagdad, but he had refused, although there was some danger from pro Axis elements. In spite of the incidence of political assassination in India in general, and in Bengal in particular, few senior Officers would allow us to take any precautions. The visits of the Supreme Commander, Mountbatten, and the Viceroy changed this. It was fortunate that I possessed a small 9 mm automatic, as I could wear this in a special holster under the skirt of my bush jacket and thus did not upset the VIP by appearing armed. The visit of Mountbatten was comparatively simple. He flew in, had a conference and lunch with Bill Slim, addressed the HQ staff and flew off again. As he only held a military appointment, the local civil authorities were in no way involved.

The Viceroy's visit was different and almost degenerated into a farce. We had been notified that he was coming not as Viceroy, but as a Field Marshal to visit Hospitals and Units in and around Comilla, and the civil authorities had been told not to lay on the customary ceremonies. The District Magistrate and Superintendent of Police were notified that the Army would provide the necessary security as the Viceroy would be travelling with Bill Slim in the GOC in C's staff car. This put Mr. Abdulla, the SP, into a panic and he came to us brandishing the official booklet on Viceroy's visits. It seemed to us that he was not so concerned for the Viceroy's safety as for his own position, for he kept reiterating that if anything happened and he had not acted strictly according to the book, he would be put out of the Police and lose his pension.

There were two bones of contention — the first was that the SP, armed, must travel in the same car as the Viceroy; this pre-supposed a Viceregal vehicle with a partition between the front and rear seats. Bill Slim's staff car was an ordinary saloon and he did not want the SP in it as it would inhibit confidential discussions, and in any event, the Viceroy would have his ADC with him, who, following normal custom, would be armed. The second was that there must be a tail car of Armed Police. The District police had no official cars so they were intending to hire a taxi. We could not reach agreement and Abdulla took the matter to Dutch, the District Magistrate and he backed the SP. A compromise was reached. Abdulla would go in the Viceroy's car, which would be proceeded by a Station Wagon in which there would be myself, the Additional Superintendent of Police and three FS NCOs, all armed, and the Police taxi would bring up the rear. The taxi was so decrepit that it broke down early in the visit and was never seen again. Otherwise the visit went off without a hitch. However in Abdulla's favour, Tippera was one of the 'bad' Districts of the thirties and one of his predecessors had been murdered by terrorists.

We were now approaching autumn and my time in 14th Army was coming to an end. The War situation throughout the world had improved considerably with the opening of the Second Front, although reports of V1 bombs dropped on London and the slow advance in front of Caen caused some anxiety. Things were going well in other theatres, but it was on our front that the most dramatic improvement had occurred. Only a month or so before, both 4 and 15 Corps had been cut off and the Japanese were besieging Kohima and threatening the plains of Assam. Now they were in full retreat; I spoke one day to one of the planning staff, who told me 'It is no longer a question of how *can* we get back into Burma but *when*. We can go in as soon as the supply situation disrupted by the Jap attacks has been restored, there is nothing now to stop us'. This return would not concern me as I had been told that I was to go back to regimental duty.

After the loss of Malaya and Burma, Churchill had castigated the Indian Army, saying publically that their arms should be given to those who would fight; the sending of three African Divisions to the Burma front was one of the results. However, the Indian Army had a champion in the Secretary of State,

Amery, who told Churchill bluntly that there was nothing basically wrong with the Army but expansion had been too rapid and, as a result, there was a serious shortage of experienced Officers and NCOs. Matters had been made worse by a large influx of Officers attached from the British Service, who, while professionally competent, had, at first, little knowledge of the customs and language of their men. He set up a Committee to examine the position and they reported that it was essential to get back to regimental duty as many regular Officers as could be spared.

Army HQ, India had asked if I could be spared, and Tony Edwardes was quite prepared to let me go, and I, also, was fed up and only too ready for a change. However before any posting was received, Tony was promoted sideways to full Colonel as Deputy Director of Transportation, and in his place came Boyes Cooper, up graded to Colonel (Intelligence). He immediately wrote off to Army HQ, that on no account could I be spared as I was probably the most experienced Security Officer of my grade in India, and further very few of the others had any knowledge of the country, the language, or the people; but to no avail. Army HQ said that the posting had been made and could not now be altered. I was relieved by a British Service Officer, Bill Talbot, of the Queen's Regiment, who had been my GSO III on the Burma Retreat, and I was posted as Second in Command of our most recently raised battalion, the 5th, situated on the Afghanistan frontier in Baluchistan, some 1600 miles away as the crow flies.

Having mentioned the influx during the War of personnel unused to the ways of the East, and India in particular, I feel that I should say something about corruption and pilfering; this had always been endemic in India. There are those who say that there was no corruption during the period of British rule but this was not so, it had always been there but the British had kept it under strict control, and thus it and petty pilfering was known as 'Dastur' or 'Custom'. The two were linked and ranged from the Rupee exacted by the doorman of the District Magistrate's Court to the percentage paid on Government contracts, and from the percentage given by the shopkeeper to your cook on all he purchased for the household to the tea and sugar which he took for his own use. The British Officer and soldier coming to India during the War looked upon all Indians as thieves, but outside the criminal classes they were inherently honest. A villager finding your wallet in the jungle would bring it in intact; my wife and I went on leave to England in the third year of Independence and we just walked out of our bungalow without locking up anything and leaving the servants in charge, and nothing was missing on our return.

The changed situation brought about by the lax moral climate during the War, the black market caused by the scarcity of many things, but particularly foodstuffs, and the run down of the administration mentioned earlier, was a fertile ground, so much so that corruption and pilfering had reached proportions which were beginning to affect the war effort. Dealing with this should have been the responsibility of the Civil and Military Police. The former were not interested and, in any event, were corrupt themselves in the lower ranks, and the latter did not really exist until 1943 and after that were very thin on the ground. No members of the (British) Corps of Military Police served in India before the war and the Corps of Indian Military Police was not raised until late 1942; up until then military policing was carried out by Regimental and Garrison Police. It was unfortunate that Security personnel should have got involved; they did not look for theft or corruption, but often this came to light during Security investigations and had to be followed up as there was no one else to whom the case could be passed.

A number of houses searched for security reasons during my time in Gauhati yielded a fair crop of stolen rations, but there were two unusual cases which came to the most unsatisfactory conclusions. The Field Security had noticed that an Artisan Works unit at Amingaon, on the north bank, were drawing their ration goats on hoof from the Gauhati Supply Depot, and taking them to the unit lines via the Pandu-Amingaon rail ferry. They were then marched some three or four miles along the river bank and back over a passenger ferry to Gauhati town where they finished in a butcher's yard. With the help of our tame Police Inspector, the FS laid on an ambush and when the goats came into the yard, they arrested the military personnel, a Jemadar and two sepoys, and the Inspector did the same for the butcher. The unit was then rung up to send an escort for their men, but instead of the escort, came the Commanding Officer, making a formal complaint to the Station Commander. The CO's story was that the Supply Depot insisted on issuing female goats, which his men would not eat, so he was selling them for the credit of unit funds. There was no doubt that the issuing of female goats to units with strong religious prejudices could cause problems, but there were a number of questions unanswered. First, it was completely illegal to sell rations for any reason whatsoever; second, had the CO complained either to the Station Commander or to the GOC?; third, why had he not refused the female goats and demanded something else in lieu, instead of this hole and corner business of selling them to the butcher, and finally, what had he done with the money, had he bought any other foodstuffs with it? I suggested that his account books be impounded to check this, but I might have been talking to a brick wall, all I and my FSO got was abuse. This did not worry us much as we were part of HQ 4 Corps and only under Gauhati Station for local administration.

The second case concerned the theft of whisky from the Station Canteen at Shillong. We had restored the check at Pandu after the 'Bats' incident and one Indian checked, carried a very heavy tin suitcase. The FS suspected a wireless, but in fact the man was a civilian canteen employee and the suitcase was full of bottles of whisky. We had the man cold; no way could he deny the theft, but I was suspicious that this might well be the tip of the iceberg, so I rang up the Station Commander at Shillong to suggest an immediate stocktaking of the Canteen be initiated, but once again we got nowhere. There was no way that we could continue our enquiries once we had brought the matter to the notice of a competent authority, and in the absense of any Military Police, this had to be Station HQ. Had we been able to hand over these cases to the SIB, they would have continued their enquiries, until they were satisfied that nothing illegal had occurred.

Two other cases I remember, which surfaced while I was in HQ 14th Army, concerned the B & A Railway. The RAF Security Liason Officer came to me one day in a great state of excitement saying that they had lost a complete wagon load of Spitfire spare parts. He was convinced that the theft was Japanese inspired, so as to immobilise the first ever Spitfire Squadron posted to the Burma front. I asked him if an escort had been sent with the wagon. He seemed amazed and replied 'No, why?' They had loaded the wagon, and then it had been locked and sealed, and the Railway Transport Officer at Calcutta had booked it to Chittagong and he had the 'Way Bill' in support of this. I was speechless at the folly of this procedure and, with some asperity, asked him if he realised that no Station nor Yard master on the B & A Railway would forward his wagon when he could get one hundred Rupees for sending on a private trader's wagon. They had been doubly foolish in not realising that there was a break of gauge between Calcutta and Chittagong, and, that without an escort to watch over the transhipment half the consignment would have been pilfered. I told him not to worry, we would find his wagon; I then asked Fort William to send out their FS from Calcutta and I would send mine from our end to check all the Yards on route. We found the wagon in a marshalling Yard about one hundred miles from its starting point and there it might have remained for the 'duration', had it not been for the Field Security.

The second episode concerned a 'racket' in the RTO's Office at Sealdah Station in Calcutta. I was not involved in this, except as a spectator, as it did not occur in my area, and, in any event, by this time the military police were reasonably well organised in Calcutta. As I have said earlier, I used to return by train after the monthly security meeting, and had a priority certificate for a reservation on the Surma Mail. This I used to present at the RTO's Office and the duty Sergeant would produce a long moan to the tune of 'Well, Sir, if you have a priority chit, I shall have to put you on, but it means putting some one else off'. The first time I travelled, I found my place was in a four berth compartment, so I sought out the reservation babu and asked him if he could change this to one in a coupé or two berth, which he did and I tipped him a rupee. There was nothing unusual or improper in this; it had long been the practice to tip the reservation babu even before the war. Later I noticed that the reservation cards had very common names — Major Jones, Captain Singh, 2/Lieut Smith and so on, and the train was not even half full. Indeed one day, I was travelling with the Deputy Director of Movements and he remarked that it was very odd that a train always reported as fully booked was so empty. I found out how the 'racket' worked. The RTO's British Clerks were in league with the reservation babus and filled up the military allotment with ficticious names. An Officer turning up for a reservation was told that there would be no places for two or three days, but if he turned up at departure time, the reservation babu might be able to fit him into the civilian allotment. The less keen types took an accomodation chit and returned to the Grand Hotel for some more leave, but the majority, the keen types turned up for the train and tipped the babu, who split the tips with the RTO's staff.

Regimental Duty— Baluchistan and Waziristan

IN August 1944 I handed over to Bill Talbot and started on the long journey to my new post. The Comilla FS Section kindly drove me down to the river port of Chandpur, thus obviating a tedious rail journey and I sailed away towards Calcutta on the Surma Mail service of steamer and train arriving there the same evening. I stayed the night with Sir Douglas and Lady Gordon and left for Lahore by the Punjab Mail the following evening. I travelled onwards from Lahore by the Karachi Mail, which had a through coach for Quetta. By the time I reached there I had been travelling the best part of a week, and still had another five or six hours to do in a local train to Chaman. However, I was spared this, as the Battalion had sent a lorry to pick me up and take me over the Khojak Pass to my destination. My experience of Indian drivers in Eastern India, many of whom appeared afraid of their vehicles, made me a little apprehensive of a journey with a Gurkha driver, who a year before had probably never seen a motor vehicle, on a hill road with sharp curves and severe gradients. I need not have worried; our Gurkha drivers certainly could drive, but with a certain 'joie de vivre', as far as speed was concerned.

The Battalion I was to join, the 5/9th Gurkha Rifles, had been raised in the summer of 1942, to avenge the loss of the

2nd Battalion at Singapore. There was an unwritten rule in the Indian Army that a unit lost through enemy action should not be re-raised during that particular campaign. To get over the loss of three Gurkha battalions, the 2/1st, 2/2nd and 2/9th, the Maharaja, the Hereditary Prime Minister of Nepal was prevailed upon to request that these Regiments should each raise a 5th Battalion, but by the autumn of 1944, none of them had gone to the Burma front, but were keeping the peace in Baluchistan.

The 5/9th was not in the highest state of military efficiency. This was due in some measure to the war time Officers, who felt that they had joined up to fight the Japanese and not to wander from garrison to garrison in Baluchistan, carrying out what appeared to be a peace time role of ensuring that the local tribesmen kept the peace. Matters were made worse by the first Commanding Officer, who, although a great gentleman, was too weak to cope with the discontented Officers, and to tell them that it was entirely up to them to get the Battalion into a fit state for war. A further factor was that there had never been a second in command who had stayed for more than a few months, before being ordered off to a command on the Burma Front. The 5/9th had only recently arived at Chaman. They had been stationed in Fort Sandeman, the Headquarters of the Zhob (frontier) Brigade, where they had fallen foul of the Brigadier, a crusty Officer from the Sikh Regiment, who did not like Gurkhas. He had reported that they were unfit to brigade with other troops and recommended their removal and the replacement of the CO. The new CO, Colonel Harry Rich of the 4th Gurkhas and I arrived almost simultaneously, and he immediately put me in charge of the two traditional functions of a Second in Command; that of Administration and the discipline of Officers. I foresaw a busy time ahead of me.

Chaman was a small garrison on the road from Quetta to Kandahar, the second city of Afghanistan; the actual Frontier and the Customs Post being situated at the end of the main street. There was a small Cantonement, comprising only the Officers quarters, Messes and the Hospital; the troops barracks were situated in four small Forts. It had been a one battalion Gurkha station, pre war, but for some reason it was now a two unit garrison. There was also a small bazaar catering largely for the lorry drivers on the Kandahar road.

The railway from Quetta had been built as a strategic line after the 2nd Afghan War, and the actual rails continued beyond the station for a hundred yards or so up to the actual frontier. It was believed that the sheds near the station contained the permanent way and other stores needed to continue the railway, the 80 or so miles to Kandahar, in the event of a war with Afghanistan. The only communication with the rest of India was by road over the Khojak Pass or by rail through the Chak Amru Range by the Shelabagh Tunnel. This tunnel was both the longest on the Indian railway system, and also the summit within it was the highest altitude reached on the Broad Gauge, over 6,000 feet. From the direction of Quetta the gradients were comparatively easy but once over the summit, the line fell down to Chaman with gradients as steep as 1 in 40. This was our lifeline, as, during the winter that I was in Chaman, the road being at a very much higher altitude was blocked by snow, often for two weeks at a time.

The Shelabagh Tunnel was very difficult to work as the steep gradients from the Chaman side necessitated three engines, and on occasions we were called upon to provide medical assistance for engine crews, who had been overcome by the fumes of the three engines working hard up into the tunnel. Sometimes the train would arrive with the train engine braking hard but with one or both of two banking engines still steaming with their crews unconscious on the footplate. The train service consisted of three passenger trains a week, but in the autumn, during the fruit season, a daily goods train was run to cater for the fruit arriving from Kandahar for distribution over much of northern India. There was no refrigerated stock, so the fruit was carried in ice bunkered vans, which gave employment to two ice factories in Chaman. The amount of fruit to be carried always exceeded the capacity of the number of vans available, so bribery was rife. There was a story that the North Western Railway administration always posted a very senior Station

Master to Chaman for his last year before retirement. In any event the noise of the arguments down at the Station could be heard all over the Cantonement.

Chaman itself being on the western side of the mountains, geographically, was not in Baluchistan at all but in Registan, a vast area of uninhabited, roadless desert, stretching away to the Afghanistan-Iran border. The cantonement was an oasis of flowers and fruit as there was plenty of water; this came by an aquaduct from springs high up in the mountains. The excellence of the gardens in the Cantonement was due to the Parsee Commanding Officer of the Hospital, Colonel Kamakarkar. This Officer, who had been commissioned before World War I, had transferred to the civil side of the Indian Medical Service, as a Civil Surgeon in Baluchistan. He was well past the age at which he could have been recalled to military duty when war came, but he volunteered with the proviso that he should be given a static job in Baluchistan. The authorities very wisely posted him to Chaman as permanent OC Hospital. As he was a permanent fixture, he was invaluable in the administration of the Cantonement and the fact that he was a keen gardener, meant that the gardens received his personal attention.

The second unit was the Bikanir Ganga Rissala (Camel Corps). This State Force Regiment was officered by a delightful body of Rajput noblemen, with whom we had the friendliest relations. Although an Imperial service unit, that is one which was available, in time of war, to reinforce the regular Indian Army, it had been very difficult to find a role for its camels. It had had some active service in the Indian Desert on the Sind-Jaisalmer border, dealing with the Hurs, a fanatical Moslem sect, who, in 1942–3 went on the rampage, attacking and looting villages, derailing and shooting up trains and generally making a great nuisance of themselves. The Regiment had been sent subsequently to Baluchistan, as the authorities thought it would be useful in semi desert conditions. The Ganga Rissala, however, thought differently, and started importuning every military HQ that they could think of to get orders to return to Bikanir. Their main argument being that the sand in Baluchistan, composed mainly of silicates was cutting the camels feet to ribbons.

One evening on my way to the Mess for dinner, they caught me out badly, I was challenged by one of their patrols, and like a fool, I had come out without my Identity Card. The Lance Daffadar (Corporal) in charge, admitted that he knew who I was, but it was only with the greatest difficulty that I was able to persuade him to release me. Finally he said 'Sahib, give me the password and you can go' Once again I was caught out, the word had been changed that day and I gave him the wrong one; so I was marched off to their Officer's Mess, and made to stand outside while the Lance Daffadar went in to report to the Adjutant. He came out grinning all over his face and said to me 'Colonel Khem Singh (the CO) says that you are a very wicked man and your punishment will be to come in and drink rum with him'. A pleasant evening followed, but I do not think I got any dinner.

The climate in Baluchistan could be very unpleasant; there was practically no rainfall, and in spite of the altitude, Quetta lying at 5,000 ft and Chaman at over 4,000 ft, the day temperature in the summer exceeded 100°F but the winters were very severe with hard frosts and snow on the mountains. The winter night temperature at Chaman for a while was as low as 0°F. I had arrived towards the end of the hot season, and I was not at all well for the first month or so. The transition from a warm damp climate at sea level to a very hot dry one at over 4,000 ft, with silicate dust thrown in, took some time to get used to. My Gurkha servant, Birman Sunwar, whom I had had since Naik Faudebehadur Mall had returned to regimental duty in early 1943, disliked it equally and in the end I had to send him back home to Shillong. The climax came at the Gurkha Festival of Dasehra; I had not gone to the celebrations as I was in bed with flu, and, when Birman arrived in the middle of the night, very drunk and complaining that the troops would give him no more rum; I decided that we must part.

The winter soon set in and after a while the road over the Pass became blocked by snow, but the railway going through the Tunnel at a lower altitude remained open. The road had only just become impassable, when two young Officers decided to go on a reconnaissance up the road in a 15 cwt truck, taking with them a wheeled carrier as escort. These wheeled carriers had a Ford chassis with a four wheel drive V8 engine, and a body of armoured plate built in the North Western Railway workshops near Lahore. They were very heavy, somewhat under engined and with a poor turning circle. It was not surprising that it stuck in the snow, and the 15 cwt truck left with the engine off while everyone tried to extricate the Carrier, suffered a cracked cylinder block. The first that we knew about this in cantonements was the return of the truck making the most ghastly noises. The crew of the Carrier had, of necessity, to be left behind, as without a guard the local tribesmen would have stripped it of everything portable. The time was now mid afternoon and it was unthinkable to leave the Carrier's crew in the snow all night. As quickly as possible a fresh Guard was detailed, kitted out in Posteens and felt boots, fed, equipped with portable oil stoves and sent up to relieve the existing Guard.

The next day the CO ordered me to recover the vehicle, and, as it appeared that it was stuck on a narrow ledge with a sharp drop on one side, the more men we had the better, so I took out two Companies. There had been further snow in the night and as we could not get a recovery vehicle right up to the spot, we marched the final mile or so, dug out the vehicle, attached drag ropes and pulled it rear first through the snow until we reached a place where it could be turned and where the recovery vehicle was waiting. Another snow adventure happened to me in a train. Orders had arrived in February that we were to be relieved in April by a State Force battalion, the Alwar Infantry and, on relief were to return to Fort Sandeman. This caused consternation amongst our Officers but Harry Rich told them bluntly that we were now a first class unit and had nothing to fear in competition with others, and, in any event, the opposition was not very formidable, being war raised battalions of the Madras and Hyderabad Regiments, and, unlike his predecessor, he was not afraid of the Brigadier. He suggested that I pay a visit to Fort Sandeman with the Quartermaster Jemadar, to discuss our arrival with the Brigade Staff.

The narrow gauge line to Fort Sandeman started from Bostan Junction, a station between Quetta and Chaman on the Quetta side of the Khojak Pass. As the trains did not connect the CO authorised me to take a vehicle to Bostan, rather than go by train from Chaman. The bitter cold of January had been replaced by mild spring like weather, but when we topped the Pass, the sky in front of us was an angry purple. The train left at about 3 p.m. on a Friday and would reach Sandeman about 11 a.m. on the next day. It returned on the following Monday. This being my first journey on this 2 ft 6 in gauge line I had come poorly provided with food, intending to rely on what the railway could furnish. I lunched at the Bostan Refreshment Room, and then had a large portion of scrambled egg put into a hot food container, which with bread and butter, I intended to have as my evening meal. Tea could be obtained at the tea stall at any station, and I would have a late breakfast or 'brunch' on arrival. The train started off on the very steep gradient which climbed to a summit over 7,000 feet, before dropping down again to Hindubagh, where at about midnight engines were changed. The snow started shortly after departure, and despite the efforts of three engines, by 10 p.m. we had still not reached the summit. The carriages on this narrow gauge line were all things considered, very comfortable given normal climactic conditions. Owing to the restricted height, each 1st Class compartment had only one transverse berth, with a bathroom opening out of it, which had a WC and wash basin fed by a force pump from underfloor tanks, but like all Indian trains no heating. The cold was intense so not long after I had eaten my supper, I decided that I would be warmer in bed, and also, as was usual in India at that time someone had stolen the electric light bulbs, the only light I had came from a hurricane lamp, which I had brought with me. I crept into my sleeping bag wearing all my clothes, battledress, leather fleece lined waistcoat, and finally I put my greatcoat on top of the sleeping bag. As the lamp gave some warmth, I left it alight, but nevertheless it was cold.

Saturday morning found us still at Hindubagh as all the engines had frozen up, and it was not until about midday that the train restarted. The snow had stopped and the sun was out, so we were comparatively comfortable, but it looked as if we would not reach our destination until after dark. However this proved to be an optimistic estimate, as about 4 p.m. the engine ran off the line. This was not a great matter as all engines carried jacks and other rerailing equipment but it now seemed probable that we should have to spend another night in a cold and foodless train. An Officer in the adjacent compartment had been invited for a weekend's shooting by the Political Agent and was bewailing the fact that he had missed one day and was likely to miss most of the next. Luckily help was at hand; as dusk set in a number of figures carrying rifles were to be seen advancing on the train, they were men of a near by Post of the para military Zhob Militia, sent by the PA to locate his guest and bring him in. He very kindly suggested that I be rescued also, so we were taken to the Post and after tea and chappatis sent on by lorry to arrive in time for a late dinner.

My return on the Monday would have been uneventful but there was an annoying occurrence. I had taken to Burma a fitted pigskin dressing case, which I had had to throw away, when I jettisoned the rest of my kit on the Retreat, retaining only the silver mounted hair brushes. Owing to a shortage of serviceable engines at Hindubagh, our train load had to be cut so that one engine only could lift it over the Pass to Bostan. My carriage was cut off, so I moved into a compartment in the other; on arrival back at Chaman, the brushes were missing; my Gurkha Orderly had left them behind at Hindubagh when transferring my kit. It was not long before I was travelling back to Sandeman; this time with the official Advance Party. I was not going to be caught out again by travelling on the Zhob Valley Railway with scanty rations, so this time and every other time, I travelled with a primus stove, kettle and frying pan, together with the wherewithal to produce tea and sausages and fried eggs.

The Military Engineering Service personnel gave me some trouble. They had alleged that when the Battalion had left for Chaman, there was a shortage of over one hundred charpoys. This was absurd but the allegation had been made possible because our war time Officers had not insisted on proper counting at the time of the hand over. After a long correspondence with higher authority, we had to pay a considerable portion of the loss, so the CO instructed me to see that there was no recurrence. The MES subordinate staff proved most obstructive, trying to get me to sign for buildings and furniture without a proper check. This I flatly refused to do and we got nearer and nearer to the day of the Battalion's arrival. The last straw was when they said that they would not work on the following day as it was a holiday. I countered this by refusing to take over the barracks and saying that I would ask Brigade HQ to erect tentage, where the Battalion could live until a proper take over was completed. The MES then capitulated and said they would do anything that I wanted. There was a sequel; two years late the MES came to redecorate my bungalow at the Infantry School, Mhow. The Superintendent of Buildings, who was in charge, was the same man who had been Superintendent of Furniture at Fort Sandeman. He did a magnificent job as I believe that he was somewhat in awe of me.

The Battalion had not been long in Fort Sandeman when the war in Europe ended and I was granted leave to England; a full two months actually in the country with air travel both ways. The most notable occurrence during my leave was that I got engaged to the Lady, with whom I have had, to date over forty very happy years. We could not get married immediately, as we were both divorced from our original spouses. I had my Decree Absolute but my future wife had only a Decree Nisi, and had some time to wait before it could be made Absolute. We agreed that she would try and come out to India the following autumn, 1946, and we would be married then. I am glad to say that neither of us changed our minds, and we were married in Agra in September 1946.

While I was in England Japan capitulated, so that when the time came for my return, all the air passages were earmarked for essential civil personnel proceeding to Burma and Malaya and I enjoyed a longer leave than I had anticipated. The India Office in mid August gave me another fortnight's Ration Cards and told me to return at the end of this period. This was repeated at two weekly intervals until the beginning of October, when we were ordered to report to a Transit Camp at Liverpool for a sea passage. Our arrival there coincided with a dock strike, so we were sent back home again. We finally sailed in early November and I got back to the Battalion, now in Wana, in mid December, just in time for Christmas. The Military Accounts Department now took a hand; Regular Officers were entitled to two months leave annually on full pay, but anything after that was Furlough on half pay. The local Headquarters of the various Officers affected put up a case that this is not applicable to them as they were ready and willing to return and it was no fault of theirs that transport could not be provided. The Accounts Department agreed the justice of this, but said they had no power to alter the Rules. The matter was finally resolved by an Order of the Governor General in Council and our pay was restored.

Wana was a frontier post in the tribal territory of South Waziristan, and very different from Chaman or Fort Sandeman. Tribal territory consisted of a mountainous strip lying between the border with Afghanistan and the administered districts of the North West Frontier Province. There was no law as far as the local inhabitants were concerned, except that they should neither take pot shots at the local garrisons, nor raid into the settled districts; rules which were more honoured in the breach than in the observance. Wana Camp could be compared to a Concentration Camp, the same barbed wire perimeter fence, watch towers and gates; the difference being that it was designed to keep the locals out rather than us in. The garrison consisted of a Brigade Group of three infantry battalions with a mountain artillery battery and mechanical and animal transport companies.

It was a non family station, indeed, no women were allowed at all. The nearby slightly larger station of Razmak had been nick named the largest 'monastery' in the world, and Wana could well be called the second largest. There was a small area around the adjacent airfield, where one could walk during daylight, otherwise no one was allowed out of the camp, except on duty and in armed parties. The road to civilisation, India, could only be used by escorted convoys on 'Road Open Days' or 'RODs' as they were usually called, when the road was picketed by the local para military force, the South Waziristan Scouts. The actual ROD date was supposed to be secret until the evening before, but, in actual fact was usually known in the camp bazaar several days before that.

Wana was unique among frontier posts in that it possessed a pack of foxhounds, the Wana Hunt, which hunted jackals on two days a week, with a mounted escort of local scallywags. It had been in existence for some years, and during the war the Army wanted to close it down, partly as being out of place in war time, and partly as few Officers had the knowledge to be the Master or Whippers in. This proposal was greeted with dismay by the Political Department, who considered that this would be taken by the locals as a sure sign that we were losing the war; so it carried on. The Master at this time was the CO of the Animal Transport Company, mainly because the kennels were in his lines and the Whippers in were the Assistant Political Officer and myself, Mounts were no problem as each battalion had two or three horses on establishment and the AT Company also had a fair number. There was no doubt that the Hunt provided a most welcome break from a boring regime as well as good exercise.

Changes were taking place in the Battalion. Even before I had gone on leave, a new Major had arrived from the 5th Gurkhas. He was a Regular, some two years senior to me in service, but luckily he was junior to me as a Major so I remained Second in Command. Later another Major arrived, this time a 7th Gurkha who had been a POW and there was no doubt of his seniority. Harry Rich did not want to lose my services as Second in Command, so he proposed that the newcomer, while being the de jure holder of the appointment and drawing the allowance, would become the Training Officer, while I would remain the de facto Second in Command. I was somewhat uneasy about this arrangement, but it seemed better than going to command a Company, where I would be the equal of the other Company Commanders, whom I had had to discipline in the past.

Not long after this, a signal was received from Army HQ appointing me as GSO II (Intelligence Co-ordination) at HQ Central Command in Agra. I think that Harry would have liked me to say that I did not want to go, and indeed, I was sorry to sever a relationship of eighteen months duration. However, I had my future to consider, so I told him that if he put up a case for my retention, I would not fight it, but I would not say that I wanted to remain. So I was warned to move to railhead at Manzai by the next ROD. As was to be expected, I was told the date by my civilian servant a day or so before it was officially announced. When the day came, I found that I was to be the Convoy Commander and that there was a suspended tow which might well delay us. The convoy itself was headed by an Armoured Car, followed by a platoon of armed soldiers in two Frontier Armoured Lorries, next some fifteen unarmed 3 tonners; this was the first half of the convoy. Then followed HQ with the reserve, this consisted of the Commander's communications truck, two Armoured Cars and two FALs. The second half followed with a rearguard of two FALs and an Armoured Car. The suspended tow was between the FALS and the Armoured Car. I had always considered that it would have been wiser to have run smaller convoys more frequently, as it would be easy for the tribesmen to ambush a vehicle in the centre of the first or second half, murder any personnel, loot it and others nearby, and then decamp before either the advance guard or the reserve could intervene. It is interesting that this was the way refugee trains were attacked in the following year.

The suspended tow was a great nuisance; it delayed us considerably at the midway halt, much to the annoyance of Officers going to join their wives on week end leave in the Cantonement of Dera Ismail Khan. When we arrived at the South Waziristan Scout's post at Jandola, a few miles from our destination, it was thirty minutes behind, and the Officers going on leave all demanded that we go on or they would miss their onward convoy. If anything went wrong, the responsibility would be mine so their demand was refused, but on hearing that there was an Armoured Car standing by, and the tow was now only fifteen minutes behind, I relented and gave the order to move on. All was well and it came in without mishap, and I had now to wait in Manzai for a day or two to catch the twice weekly train to Mari Indus en route to Lahore.

The VIP quarter in the transit block was allotted to me as the senior Officer travelling, and better still I was allowed to sleep in the train during the night before a 5 a.m. departure. Manzai, although a railhead, was in tribal territory, so the station was inside the perimeter of the camp, and the incoming train had to halt outside for a strict search before being allowed in. The next morning I left Manzai and arrived in Agra on the 11th of February 1946.

CHAPTER SIX

The Political and Military Scene

THE political events in India had passed me by during my sojourn on the Frontier, but now, as my new job was likely to be dominated by these same events, I had a lot of catching up to do. It was ironic that at last I was to be employed in the type of work for which I had been recommended at my Intelligence Course. During the winter of 1944–5, the political scene had been stagnant as the Congress leaders were in jail, but there was a change in March 1945, when the Moslem League Ministry in the North West Frontier Province was defeated and a Congress Ministry, under one of the few leaders not in prison, took office. This was the first Congress Ministry to return to power since they had resigned en bloc at the outbreak of war.

The situation then was that responsible Government existed in six of the eleven Provinces — Moslem League in Bengal and Sind, a coalition, in which the league was the senior partner, in Assam, the Unionists (a non religious landowners party) in the Punjab, a Hindu 'anti Congress' Ministry in Orissa, and finally a Congress Ministry in the NWFP. All the other Provinces were under the direct rule of their respective Governors.

Those with responsible Governments, although in the majority, only included two of any political importance, Bengal and the Punjab, while the three large and politically important Provinces of Bombay, Madras and the United Provinces were still under direct rule.

The country had been quiet during this time and both the Viceroy, Wavell, and the Commander in Chief, Auchinleck had won great respect from many shades of Indian opinion. The end of the war now being in sight, the Viceroy in June 1945 persuaded a somewhat reluctant British Government to allow him to release the Congress leaders and to call a constitutional conference at Simla. This conference, composed of representatives of all parties, was intended to ratify the Viceroy's proposal for a new representative Viceroy's Council in which only himself and the Commander in Chief would be official members, all other portfolios would be held by Indian politicians. It was hoped also that proposals for a new Constitution could be formulated.

Much to the chagrin of the Viceroy, the conference was a complete failure. The stumbling block was parity in the new Council between the Congress and the Moslem League. The Congress insisted that they should nominate all the Hindu members and even one or two Congress Moslems, together with the member representing the 'Scheduled Castes'. The League would have none of this and insisted that they nominate all the Moslem members, disregarding the claims of the Unionist Moslems from the Pubjab. None of this was acceptable to the Viceroy, and the Conference broke up. The Congress then started a campaign of inflammatory speeches directed against Indian Government servants and police. The object was to intimidate these people so greatly by threats of legal action after Independence that they would be rendered useless for further service and thus bring about a collapse of the administration. One of the most effective threats was that all officials who had taken part in the suppression of the '42 Uprising would be put on trial as 'war criminals'.

The Viceroy, undaunted, quietly went ahead with his plan to restore responsible rule in all the Provinces by announcing that elections would be held in the forthcoming winter, but until then there would be no change in the Viceroy's Council; all but three official members and one of the nominated, were Indians anyway. However before anything concrete could be achieved the political scene was thrown into turmoil by the trial of the leaders of the 'Indian National Army'. About one third of all Indian Officers and men captured by the Japanese in Malaya, Hongkong and Burma, about 20,000, had defected, but the majority had done so to avoid starvation and torture rather than an actual desire to re-enter the fight against their old comrades or to promote Indian Independence.

The greatest secrecy had obtained over the capture of such personnel, and it was not until after the Japanese surrender that the Indian public had become aware that the Japanese had any Indian soldiers fighting for them. The problem now was what was to be done with them. The first and very sensible decision was that they should be segregated under guard, and after interrogation, sorted out into three categories — 'black', who would be put on trial — 'grey', who would be discharged, and 'white', who would be returned to their units. It was heartening that the majority were in the latter category. The next problem was to decide under which section of Military Law should charges be brought against the 'blacks'; it was obvious that they had waged war against the King Emperor, but so had the 'greys' and the 'whites'. The main factor in bringing these men to trial was that many had used appalling brutality in coercing their comrades into the INA, and those, who had remained loyal were crying out for justice, and who could blame them.

With hindsight it is now considered that a serious error of judgement was made in staging a show trial in the Red Fort at Delhi of three of the ringleaders, all ex Officers and comprising a Hindu, a Sikh and a Moslem. It was doubtful if these men had acted with brutality towards their comrades and, indeed, two of the defendants were acquitted of this charge, but all three were found guilty of wageing war against the King Emperor, and sentenced to be cashiered and to terms of transportation. Both the Viceroy and the Commander in Chief, who were being inundated with advice from all quarters, were in a quandary as to whether the sentences should be confirmed or not. Finally it was decided that the sentence of transportation should be remitted.

The whole affair engendered great excitement throughout the country, and the, perhaps, misguided selection of a Hindu, a Moslem and a Sikh meant that no political party could stand aloof. The trial venue of the Red Fort in Delhi, the symbol of British power, was probably unwise. Great damage had been done on the political front and disturbances broke out in many Cities, culminating, in Calcutta, with a full scale anti Government riot. Many moderate Indians could not understand why these persons had been brought to trial at all, when their only crime was to desire Indian Independence, something which had been promised anyway. The leniency of the sentences dismayed many of the loyal Officers and soldiers. To make the best of a very difficult situation, the decision was made that, in the future, only those accused of gross brutality would be tried; the others quietly discharged.

The War had been over for sometime, although there were still Indian troops on active service overseas, keeping the peace between warring factions; mainly in Greece and Indonesia. The chief factors of the military scene in India were 'Aid to the Civil Power' and 'Demobilisation'. The two were not compatible as the fewer the troops available the more difficult the task of keeping the peace became. There was a great difference and the attitude of British and Indian troops to demobilisation; the average British soldier wished to get out as soon as possible, the Indian to stay in, if possible as a regular soldier. The demobilisation, therefore, of Indian soldiers posed few problems; most were cultivators who would return to their family holdings. Both Wavell and Auchinleck had done a great deal in getting the Provincial Governments to organise resettlement schemes for ex soldiers.

The position of the British servicemen was quite different, not only did they wish to return to civilian life, but more important they wished to return to England. Their response to the Indian shouts of 'Quit India' was 'as soon as possible'.

There had been widespread disturbance, amounting in some cases to outright mutiny, at the end of World War I. This was due to the unfair system of demobilisation, whereby a man conscripted in 1918 could get out before another who had joined voluntarily in 1914, if his employer stated that his return was essential. The system at the end of World War II was one of points giving equal weightage to length of service and age. This was not only inherently fair, but enabled reasonably accurate forecasting as to when a particular points group would be released. The result was that morale was high and no incident occurred in the Army, but regrettably some did amongst RAF personnel stationed in India. Morale was equally high in the Indian Army, although three minor cases of indiscipline did occur. Morale was not so high in the Royal Indian Navy and Royal Indian Air Force for a variety of reasons, and here there were some major incidents.

To summarise — when I took up my new duties, the country was in a fairly disturbed state, the political position very volatile, but the Army, British and Indian was in good heart.

CHAPTER SEVEN

Settling in — the Mutinies

M Y arrival in Agra was on the 11th February, both a day and a month of ill omen, as it was on that day that the Calcutta Riots started and later in the month the Royal Indian Navy staged a full scale Mutiny.

I was alloted a quarter in 'B' Mess. HQ Central Command had three Officer's Messes, catering for all from Colonels down, and B Mess comprised a large bungalow for the Mess proper and a number of hutments divided into single quarters. These were not uncomfortable at that time of year but, even with fans, were likely to be very hot and stuffy in temperatures of 110–115 in the high summer. This Mess had the advantage of being in a very pleasant part of the Cantonement, close to the Club and Bazaar, but it was nearly two miles from the old British barracks in which the Headquarters were situated; a not very pleasant bicycle ride in the hot weather.

The GOC in C was my old Commander from Assam, General Scoones and the BGS, a British Service Officer, Brigadier Ellenberger. I soon found out the reason for having a GSO II 'Intelligence Co-ordination'. The original structure of the General Staff was one of four sections — Operations, Intelligence, Training and Staff Duties, the latter almost entirely taken up with disbandment of redundant units. The Operations section had a relatively minor role, that of Internal Security so it was combined with Intelligence under a GSO I (Operations and Intelligence); the Operations sub section having a GSO II, Intelligence a GSO III I(a) and a GSO II I(b). Unfortunately the GSO I (Ops & I), although a well known Intelligence

Officer, was an expert on China and had little knowledge of the Indian political scene. The General wished to get rid of him, but thought this would be difficult, so, with some cunning, he said that the Staff structure was wrong; the two sections should be separated, and two GSO IIs, as Section Heads, should replace the GSO I (Ops & I). This meant that there would be two GSO IIs in Intelligence, one as Senior Intelligence Officer and section head, and the other in charge of I(b). Someone had the bright idea of calling the senior, GSO II (Intelligence Co-ordination). This was nonsense as he was the 'boss' and not a co-ordinator. It proved to be an arrangement which was not entirely satisfactory.

The GSO II I(b), Bill Moorshead, was considerably older than I; he had been a Battery Sergeant Major in the Royal Artillery, who had married an Anglo Indian girl and taken his discharge in India to join the Bengal Police as a Sergeant in the Chittagong Armed Section. He gained a King's Police Medal for his service with his all Gurkha armed police during the Chittagong Armoury Raid in 1930. He later transferred to the Calcutta Armed Police, also Gurkha, where he was promoted Inspector. He was very efficient and knowledgeable in Security work, and he and his wife were very pleasant people. The GSO III, Hurst, from my own Regiment, was a Karachi graduate who ran his section to my satisfaction.

There was no time to settle down before trouble started. India was beginning to slide slowly and surely into chaos. On the actual day of my arrival, a major riot broke out in Calcutta; more serious than anything which happened for some time. It lasted for three days and overflowed into the shopping and business quarters, where a number of Europeans were assaulted; indeed any one wearing western style dress was liable to have his hat knocked off or his tie pulled. It took two British and one Gurkha Battalion to restore order; fire being opened several times on the mobs.

A week later the Royal Indian Navy in Bombay and Karachi erupted into open and violent mutiny. Earlier there had been unrest in a number of RAF stations in India, and, perhaps, unwisely, the authorities took no action as the indiscipline was called a 'strike'; a refusal to parade, work or take food, without any violence. The Royal Indian Air Force was largely integrated with the RAF so the 'strike' spread to their men also. The RIN enlisted the same educated technical personnel as the RAF so the lack of any disciplinary action against the latter encouraged the former. It was fortunate that the Petty Officers remained loyal, and that, in Bombay, the sailors were prevented from taking over the armouries. Even so the trouble there lasted three days, but luckily both the men in the Naval Barracks and those coming ashore from ships in the harbour were prevented by troops from breaking out into the town. The Congress leaders took fright at the violence and advised the mutineers to surrender, sending one of their most senior members, Sardar Patel, to Bombay to mediate.

The events in Karachi were more serious and culminated in a full scale battle between a ship firing its complete armament, including 4 in guns and the troops replying with rifles, mortars, machine guns and even a 75 mm howitzer. The trouble was caused by domestic grievances fanned by the explosive political climate.

The Army had no incidents in British units and only three relatively minor ones in Indian units. One, a very low key incident, involving a Pioneer unit, was in Calcutta, but the other two were in Central Command, and were an introduction to my new duties. Some incidents of indiscipline had occurred in a Mahratta battalion, while travelling by train from Bombay Docks to Kamptee, the cantonement of Nagpur. This was a curious case which we could never unravel. The battalion had landed at the time of the Naval Mutiny, and could not fail to notice the general air of excitement, with loudspeakers blaring and shots being fired. They were ordered to lay out their kits on the quay for Military Police and Customs inspection; a normal and necessary duty, but one much resented by troops returning from active service. A Gurkha battalion followed them off the ship, but, for lack of space, were marched to another venue for their inspection. It will never be known what exactly went on in the minds of the Mahrattas, but evidently something that they had seen or some stories that they had been told fermented in their brains. It may be that they thought that the Gurkhas were getting preferential treatment, but, whatever the cause, there were cases of indiscipline in one Company during the journey to Kamptee. If any military action had had to be taken, the only unit available there was the Regimental Centre of the newly raised Mahar Regiment. Mahars were low caste people of the Mahratta region, who in the past had suffered at the hands of caste Mahrattas. They were secretly hoping that they would be called out to deal with any trouble, which greatly upset the Mahratta Chief Minister of the Central Provinces. He loosed off a battery of telegrams to The Viceroy, Commander in Chief, and GOC in C Central Command. Luckily the errant company was contained by the rest of the Battalion so the Chief Minister could have saved himself much anxiety.

Not long after this trouble errupted during the Victory Parade in New Delhi. The marching columns were hooted at and even stoned during their progress, and while the police were busy in protecting them the goondas rioted in Old Delhi and burnt the Town Hall. About this time, the most serious of the Army disturbances took place — a Mutiny at the Indian Signals Centre at Jubbulpore. This was caused by a number of legimate grievances, aggravated by poor administration and man-management. The Signals had recruited, pre war, the usual martial classes, but war time expansion had filled the ranks with a large number of Madrassis, whom the north Indians despised. The natural consequence of the expansion was north Indian VCOs and NCOs with Madrassi other ranks, and cases of discrimination and friction were legion. Many of the junior British Officers, seconded from the Royal Corps of Signals, had only recently been posted to India and neither knew or greatly cared for their men. An explosive situation built up and the overbearing attitude of the PM Subedar Major to Madrassis on the question of leave was sufficient to light the fuse. Energetic measures to restore discipline and full enquiries into the men's grievances succeeded in restoring order, and no further trouble occurred, nor did it in any other unit.

The Signals Mutiny resulted in a shakeup of General Staff Branch and the posting out of the BGS. Brigadier Ellenberger had refused my request to proceed to Jubbulpore to get to the root of things; instead he kept me enciphering personally Top Secret Signals to Army HQ. Matters came to a head after about a week, when I was asked by the General for a resume of what had happened, and what were the causes and possible remedies; I had to answer that I knew very little about it. This provoked a roar from the General who then asked me whether I had been to Jubbulpore; my negative reply made matters worse and, on being asked why, I could reply — 'because the BGS would not let me go!' The next to be interrogated was the Assistant Adjutant General, a very experienced Indian Army Officer; he, also, had to confess to knowing or doing very little on the discipline or morale angle. His excuse was a valid one — 'because General Staff branch did not keep me informed.' By now it was obvious that heads would roll, but actually only one did, Brigadier Ellenberger's. He was replaced by Brigadier 'Tochi' Barker, a 2nd Goorkha, the same Regiment as the General.

General Staff Branch now settled down with two first class Officers. General Scoones was not generally popular as he demanded very high standards, but he was fair and, as he had been at one time Head of Intelligence at Army HQ, he had a soft spot for the Intelligence Branch, provided it did not make too many mistkaes. Tochi Barker, had come from the 43rd Gurkha Lorried Brigade, which he had led in the latter stages of the Italian campaign. He had been accused by some of his subordinates of being wasteful of his men's lives, but I found him a very helpful and considerate 'boss'.

Agra, besides being a well laid out and spacious Cantonement, had many places of interest dating from the time of the Mogul Emperors. The most famous was the Taj Mahal, followed by the Fort, an enormous area enclosed by a red sandstone wall, which was both a defended area and a Palace. There were other places in the vicinity, notably Sikandra Bagh, the tomb of the Emperor Akbar, the ruined city of Fatehpur Sikri, and the lovely shrine of Itmad-ad-Daulat. The difficulty was transport, cars were still unobtainable, so the only way of getting about was bicycle or tonga.

This problem was solved shortly after my arrival. I found an Officer who had a horse for sale. This animal was a 20th Lancer troop horse, made redundant by mechanisation, and besides being an excellent ride was trained to go in harness. These redundant horses were known as '100 chippers', because they had been sold originally to Officers at one hundred Rupees, and could only be resold for the same sum. There was also a trap with its harness for sale, so the seller naturally put up the price of these items to compensate for the relatively low price he was getting for the horse, but I now had not only a horse to ride but also a means of transport.

I had not driven before, although I was a fully competent rider, but I found this skill not too difficult to acquire. The first time I drove to office, I had an amusing encounter with the Major General Administration, General Dyer, a Cavalry Officer, and one who many years later was to be the President of the Indian Army Association when I was its Chairman. I had just turned into the HQ area, when I saw a 'flagged' Staff Car behind me; it came to a halt and out jumped the General. I had visions of a ticking off for holding him up, but not so. He rushed up, had a look at the wheel hubs and then said 'I thought so, made by Johns & Company of Agra about 1900'.

Both the horse and the trap were a great joy; not only could I go to and from my work, but my bearer could bring my lunch, obviating a hot and tedious drive to and from the Mess. In the evening I had a choice of a ride or a drive to the Taj Mahal or to the Cinema or Bazaar. The Assistant Military Secretary, Colonel 'Orlando' Holland, another Cavalry Officer, also had a horse, and he invited me to join a sort of riding club of the four or five of us with horses. The General's daughter, and, sometimes, the General, himself, rode with us and we were usually invited to his house for drinks at the conclusion of the ride.

Now that the Mutinies were over, I had a chance to settle into my job and take stock of the political and military situation in the Command. The area for which I was responsible was immense, about four times the size of the United Kingdom and with a population of 108 million. It comprised about one half of the Punjab, that is all to the east of the Ravi river, and included the capital, Lahore, the whole of the United and Central Provinces, and a large number of Native States. The CP and the Native States would pose few political and security problems, but not so the Punjab and the UP. The former was moving fast to a serious Moslem-Hindu confrontation, with the Sikhs thrown in for good measure, while the latter was one of the major strongholds of the Congress Party, as well as having a very considerable Moslem minority.

This area was organised into three military 'Areas', a Major General's command, Lahore, Lucknow and Nagpur, corresponding roughly to the three Provinces. Each Area was subdivided into several 'Sub Areas' each under a Brigadier. I reckoned that there were fifteen major military stations scattered about the Command, without counting smaller ones, hill stations and so on. The whole set up was quite different from that in Assam or in 14th Army, where everything was much more concentrated.

While I had been away at regimental duty, things had altered radically in the organisation of Intelligence; now all Officers in Intelligence appointments were attached to the Indian Intelligence Corps, and the Senior Intelligence Officer in each Army or Command was made the de facto 'Commander Intelligence Corps'. This meant that I was responsible to a certain degree for the three GSOs III in the Areas, and the Intelligence Officers in the Sub Areas, and I had the power to switch them about in appointments within the Command. I was also in a way the General's political adviser, and had the right of access to him in an emergency without going through the BGS. I had to attend his office at 9 am every morning to give him the daily news. This entailed reading several national and local newspapers, listening to the morning All India Radio News, as well as digesting any reports from the three Areas. I found this impossible to do, if I was to have breakfast in the Mess, so my bearer brought it to my room, and I ate while reading the papers and listening to the Radio.

There were certain difficulties bound up with my rank. It took some time for my position to be recognised; the Signals Branch, for example, treated me as an ordinary second grade staff officer. Matters came to a head, when in the course of an exercise to test communications, I was hauled up in front of the General as the result of a signal which I had never seen. The HQ had been out of touch with Lucknow Area most of the night as a result of atmospherics, and at 'morning prayers', the daily conference, I mentioned this when giving my report on the general situation. I was sent for later by the General and found him and the BGS studying a signal. The former said in a very irate tone of voice "You said that we had received nothing from Lucnow, well, what is this?' I naturally replied that I had never seen the signal, on which Tochi said that it was on the Operations Room information board. I could see my return to Regimental duty looming up, but I replied, with some heat, that as Senior Intelligence Officer, I had no time to go reading signals on the Ops Room Board, and, further, it was my duty to study and evaluate such pieces of information before showing them to the General and BGS. This required the peace and quiet of my office rather than fighting for a glimpse of them in the crowded Ops Room.

The General quietened down and sent for the Chief Signals Officer, who produced an Order that personal copies of Signals were only given to 1st Grade Officers. Thus in General Staff Branch, the GSOs I Training and Staff Duties would receive them but not the GSO II Operation or myself; the staff officers vitally concerned. Further, personal copies of Signals were given to such obscure beings as the Colonel (Legal) and the Colonel (Catering). The General's ill advised re-arrangement of the staff structure had put both the GSO II (Operations) and myself at a disadvantage as a in a a big HQ, there were a large number of senior Officers, who did not realise that we were Heads of the two most important sections of the General Staff, although only GSO IIs. This was reversed in my case when I went on tour to liase with the Provincial Governments, there I dealt with the Chief Secretary and Inspector General of Police as the General's Political and Security Adviser.

I had a further passage with the General in the Ops Room. One afternoon during an exercise, he came in and spotting a British Other Rank in the background, asked him what he knew, and got the surprising reply — 'Don't know nothing about it, Sir, I'm properly cheesed off'. Of course the General took this man to be one of my clerks, and gave me a ticking off, before I could explain that he was nothing to do with us, but an RAF clerk, who had come with their Liaison Officer.

Bill Moorshread and Hurst were a good team but the position regarding Intelligence Officers and clerical staff was very unsatisfactory. The former were very hard to get, the war was over and there was little glamour in the position of an IO in a large static HQ. Army HQ were reluctant to employ Indian Officers in Intelligence, and this narrowed the field. Finally we got an Anglo Indian junior WAC(I) officer, who was reputed to be trained in Intelligence, but she was a disaster. A very attractive girl, she was lazy to a degree, and not even a chasing up by the Commander WAC(I) of the Command could get her working so she had to go. The clerical position was equally bad. The Indian Army Corps of Clerks pre war was a highly efficient body, split into British ranks for General Staff and civilian Indians for the other Branches, Army HQ refused to allow Indian clerks in GS(I) Branch, so, we were dependent on the British Staff Sergeants and WOs I. Recruitment pre war was from Orderly Room Sergeants and Corporals of British Regiments in India, men of some service and experience of office routine; competition was fierce as the successful candidate was made immediately a Staff Sergeant, and at the end of his year's probation promoted to Sub Conductor, a WO I. This ensured a very high standard. War time expansion appreciably lowered the standard as very a large number of clerical personnel were required in the new HQs set up. The new entry were either young British soldiers or directly recruited Anglo Indian youths; few of either category had much experience of office routine, nor the status to support a Warrant Officer's rank. Our Superintendent Clerk in 'I' was a young soldier, made up to Warrant rank, likeable and willing, but in no way fit for the job of running the office of an important section of the General Staff.

Another headache was the lack of a stenographer. I represented to the BGS, that one was essential in view of the number of Intelligence Summaries and Appreciations that were required. None could be found amongst the British clerks, and I was precluded from having an Indian, although there were many who could take dictation. A rather ridiculous compromise was effected; I could not have an Indian from the Army's Corps of Clerks but I could have one from the Police, so a civilian member of clerical staff of the District CID was seconded to our Intelligence Branch.

I made a number of friends, British and Indian, during my time in Central Command; but two require special mention, regrettably both now dead; One was my old friend and former boss, Philip Gwyn, who was Colonel 'Q', which seemed a curious appointment for a senior Intelligence Officer and a Japanese interpreter. He had been Brigadier (Intelligence) in HQ Allied Land Forces, South East Asia, but had been sacked when Oliver Leese on taking command, got ride of all Indian Army personnel, and replaced them by British Service Officers, whom he had brought with him. Should we have any queries which 'Q' Branch might answer, Philip was always ready to help. The other was my opposite number in Operations, Donald Addison, of the Royal Tank Regiment, Donald had been severely wounded in the Desert, where he won an MC; many said that he should have received a higher award. He had been sent to staff jobs in India as he was medically unfit for active service, and he was an extremely competent and hard working Staff Officer, as well as a delightful person to work with. After retirement he and his wife came to live near us so our friendship continued until their respective deaths. His job could have better named 'Internal Security' rather than 'Operations'. It was here that his lack of knowledge of India and, particularly, its geography, put him at a disadvantage, but he very quickly overcame this difficulty.

CHAPTER EIGHT

Plan 'Asylum' — The Cabinet Mission

A<small>RMY</small> Headquarters naturally viewed with concern the mounting waves of violence and the increasingly inflammatory speeches of the politicians. They ordered each Command to prepare a plan which would not only counter outright rebellion, but would provide protection for Europeans and Government servants in that event. This was given the code name of 'Plan Asylum'. We were told to be prepared for something even more serious than the 1942 uprising, and to be ready to deal with it by every means in our power, including the use of Armoured forces and Aircraft.

Our plans envisaged the rapid movement of forces, as required, from one end of the Command to the other, and as the railways were easy to sabotage, the bulk of the movement would have to be by road. The pre war 'route books' were out of date as they had been produced for marching infantry and cavalry and not for mechanised columns or tanks, and to complicate matters the civilian PWD's method of classifying bridges was different to the Army's. We had six major rivers in the Command — the Ravi, Beas and Sutlej in the Punjab, the Ganges and Jumna in the UP and the Chambal in the south, to say nothing of numerous tributaries, so it was obvious that the bridges on all the major roads would have to be re-surveyed. East to west was well covered by good roads with all the rivers bridged, but the construction of some of the larger bridges presented problems. Partly for economy and partly to facilitate protection, these bridges were double deckers, with the railway on the top deck and the road below. Each was protected by steel gates across both rail and road, with blockhouses incorporated at either end; the gates across the railway were straight forward, but those across the road were at right angles. This meant that vehicles had to enter through a narrow gate into the blockhouse and then make a right angled turn on the bridge proper. This precluded the movement of tanks on transporters and, probably, even tanks themselves. It might be necessary to take them over on railway flats, which would cause severe delays.

The two roads to the south, the Bombay-Agra between Agra and Gwalior, and the Cawnpore-Jhansi lacked permanent bridges over the Chambal and Jumna Rivers respectively. A bridge of boats sufficed until the advent of the monsoon, when it was removed and replaced by a manually operated ferry capable of taking only one car or lorry at a time, and even this was suspended when the river was in spate. Luckily, we were able to use the nearby railway bridges, which had been decked for use in an emergency, but the railway administration looked upon this as a great nuisance and were inclined to be unhelpful. For example — the great bridge over the Jumna on the Cawnpore-Jhansi line was approached by long and high embankments, which made the road approach very difficult, and to further complicate matters, the railway authorities required each road convoy to be signalled as if it were a train, and to carry two railwaymen equipped with lamps, flags and detonators to protect the line in case of a breakdown.

We had other headaches, but the most taxing one was the protection of Europeans and Government servants. All the existing internal security schemes specified evacuation to a 'strong point', which was usually the 'Fort' and practically every District had one. This may have worked at the time of the Great Mutiny, but the number of Government servants alone, had risen to such an extent, that the various Forts would never have contained them, to say nothing of being able to provide food, water, and sanitation for such a throng. A further difficulty was where to draw the line; were Anglo Indians to be evacuated as Europeans and to what level did the category of Government servant apply? Were lower grade railway or hospital employees to be evacuated? An encampment with defences large enough to contain all and sundry would have been almost impossible to construct, and quite impossible to keep secret. The Plan itself was supposed to be a strict secret, but, of course, parts of it leaked out. The leakages came from practically every military Headquarters, to say nothing of those from the civilian authorities. Portions of the Plan, sometimes authentic and sometimes pure fantasy, appeared constantly in the nationalist Press and the Congress, in particular, made political capital out of it; their theme was — if the British were going to hand over power no such plan would be necessary, so all moves towards Independence were but a pretence, designed as delaying tactics until the British felt themselves strong enough to take action.

The Plan, however, remained in being and various preparations were made, although they were never used for the purpose for which they had been designed. This was because, from July onward, the emphasis shifted away from anti Government activity to communal. The level of violence and disorder increased by leaps and bounds but it was the communities attacking each other rather than the Government. Emphasis must be given to the fact that any successful action would have depended on the loyalty of hundreds of thousands of Indians in the Army, Civil Service and Police.

The general feeling, from the Viceroy down, was that the Indian soldier, in spite of the INA excitement was untouched by the general political feeling and could be relied on to be entirely loyal, and this probably would be true of the Indian element of the Officer Corps. Most of the Indian Officers were nationalist at heart, but realised the necessity of a non political army and of a calm, smooth handover, which only the Army could ensure. This and their training would keep them loyal. The Police and lower Government servants were in a different category, because they were too close to the general public to be entirely unaffected, and it would have been difficult for them not to be involved in the waves of industrial unrest that were beginning to manifest themselves all over the country. Indeed, during my time in the Command we had a national postal strike, and a railway strike was only called off at the eleventh hour; sporadic four hour stoppages and go slows were endemic on all railways during the period. The Anglo Indian staff, although continuing loyal, were beginning to look over their shoulders and wonder what their position would be after any hand over of power.

The elections for the Provincial Assemblies ran true to form in most areas. The Congress captured all the Hindu majority Provinces, with Assam reverting to Congress rule. Things were not so straight forward in those with a Moslem majority; the Moslem League retained power in Bengal and Sind, but Congress was returned in the Frontier Province. The main upset was in the Punjab, where the situation was confused. The Unionist Party which had ruled since 1937, was reduced to a handful, winning only about ten seats. This was probably because the original leaders of the Party, the Moslem, Sir Sikander Hyat Khan Tiwana, and the Hindu, Sir Chottu Ram had died and the present Chief Minister, Sir Khizr Hyat Khan was not of the same calibre as Sir Sikander, his predecessor. The Moslem League swept home in practically all the Moslem constituencies, but they were just short óf an overall majority. Khizr clung tenaciously to office and was able to form a Ministry in alliance with the Congress. The League reacted angrily because they considered, as the majority party, the Governor should have given them a chance to form a Ministry. There is a body of opinion that the Governor should have done this; had they been unable to form a Government, or even having formed one, been defeated in the Assembly, at least it could be said that they had been given the opportunity. However, as it turned out, there was now a non Moslem Government in a Moslem majority province and the League raised the cry that they had been betrayed. Much of the later holocaust in the Punjab can be traced back to these events. We were able to forecast the Punjab result correctly, which was a great feather in our caps as the General had been assured by the Governor of a Unionist victory.

The British Government becoming alarmed at events and the lack of any progress towards Congress-League accord, dispatched in late March a 'Cabinet Mission' to try and formulate a plan for an orderly hand over of power. The Mission was an ill assorted trio; the leader, Lord Pethick Lawrence, had no experience of India and was too old to understand the intricacies of Indian politics; Sir Stafford Cripps, well briefed by the Congress unofficial envoy in Britain, Krishna Menon, was blatantly partisan in his approach and often went behind the Viceroy's back to negotiate direct with the Congress, which provoked grave suspicion in League circles; only Mr. A. V. Alexander, made a real effort to appreciate the difficulties and to be fair to all parties.

The Mission was inundated with representations from every political or religious party or sect, but it was obvious that only two counted, the Congress and the Moslem League, and their positions were poles apart. The Congress were adament that India should become a single secular democratic State, while the League was equally firm that they would never submit to Hindu rule and thus, the Moslem majority areas in the North West and North East should be detached to form Pakistan, a separate sovereign Moslem State. The League proposal went further than the Mission could agree to in fairness to the Hindus in the Punjab and Bengal, where the Moslem majority was not large, by Indian standards — 16 million Moslems to 12 million Hindus in the Punjab and 33 million to 27 million in Bengal, while in Assam the Hindus were in the majority. The Mission informed Jinnah, the League President, that should he persist in pressing for a sovereign independent state, the eastern half of the Punjab and the western half of Bengal, together with Assam less Sylhet District could not be included. Jinnah refused this and the negotiations once again reached deadlock.

The Mission then produced an ingenious three tier system — a Central Government with the very limited powers of Defence, Foreign Affairs and Communications; the Provinces to deal with all other aspects of government, but sandwiched in between the right of Provinces to form 'Group' Governments and

'Group' Legislatures. To allay Moslem fears of a Hindu dominated Central Government, it was proposed that the Hindu and Moslem Groups of Provinces should have equal representation in the Central Legislature.

Failing to get agreement on these proposals, the Mission issued them as a 'fait accompli' and at the same time the Viceroy issued his proposals for a new Council, the Indian Cabinet, in which he would be the only European or Official, even the Commander in Chief, would be replaced by an Indian Defence Minister. The proposed composition was five Congress, five League, one Sikh, one Parsee, one Indian Christian and one other, the highly respected Madras Hindu, Mr. Rajagopalachari, later to become President of India. The Plans were very well received in the country, even Gandhi expressed the view that they were the best solution in the circumstances, but the Congress and the League continued to haggle.

The League, however, came to the conclusion that this solution was the best that they were likely to achieve and agreed to both the three tier system and the new Council. Actually they were doing very well; the three tier system would give them a Moslem block in both the North West and North East, and in the latter they would command India's largest industrial area, Bengal. They would receive, also, two major ports, Calcutta and Karachi as well as the smaller one of Chittagong. The two Hindu Provinces lying between — the UP and Bihar — contained the largest Moslem minorities, and, by reason of culture and language, the Moslems had great influence. In effect, there would be an area of Moslem influence lying across the whole of north India. The Congress continued to procrastinate, but finlly on the 26th of June they agreed the two plans, but with reservations regarding the Council. The Mission then left India with high hopes that something concrete had been achieved, but their hopes were soon dashed. First, Gandhi disrupted the discussions by insisting on the inclusion of a Congress Moslem in the Government, something which Jinnah would not agree to, then the Viceroy losing patience with both sides postponed any idea of a popular Government until both sides could agree. He announced a caretaker Council of officials, of which only two were Indians, both members of the ICS. The Viceroy's decision enraged Jinnah, who considered that he had the right to form a Government of the League if the Congress refused to co-operate. In spite of this, success was near as the All India Congress Committee agreed the two Plans, but three days later, Nehru put everything back into the melting pot, by telling a news conference that the Congress had only agreed proposals for a Constituent Assembly and were free to modify the three tier Plan and the new Government as they thought fit. The Congress Working Committee disassociated themselves from Nehru's utterances and reiterated their support for both Plans, but the damage had been done. Jinnah decided that no reliance could be placed on a body, which could neither make up its mind nor abide by its undertakings. There could only be one solution now for the League — an independent Pakistan, even if they had to resort to violence to get it.

CHAPTER NINE

Alarms and Excursions — Communal Violence

THE situation in August 1946, when India was about to enter the last year of British rule might be described as the year of 'fire and slaughter'. The two communities were as far apart as ever, and the British Government was still committed to hand over power to a single Central Government. It was difficult to envisage a more potentially critical situation.

The Congress was in a strong position as they controlled all but two of the Provinces, although they were only the senior partner of a coalition in the Pubjab, and in the NWF Province it was doubtful if, even with a Congress Government, the local Pathans would support Hindus in a fight against other Moslems. They were beginning to be more moderate in their demands and to gain the confidence of the smaller communities, who were now ready to co-operate with them in an Interim Government. They were still committed to an undivided India. Time was the enemy. How long would they wait while the Viceroy attempted to cajole the League into supporting the three tier system. The League's position, however, was appallingly weak. They only controlled two provinces — Bengal and Sind, and in spite of energetic efforts to get Bengali Moslems to settle in Assam only Sylhet district had a Moslem majority. While they had an overall majority in Bengal, they only counted for 23% of the population of Calcutta, and it was unlikely that, in view of this, Congress would surrender India's chief port and industrial city. The position in the traditionally Moslem north west was worse, with only Sind having a League Ministry and Congress controlling the Punjab and the NWFP. Jinnah was in a very ugly frame of mind and was determined to show the British Government and, indeed the world, that come what may there would be a State of Pakistan, even if he had to make parts of India ungovernable to get it.

The sole hope of keeping the peace was a strong Government, but sadly the administration was grinding to a halt. Many British members of the Indian Civil Service and Indian Police Service were leaving the country, either on retirement or on leave after the war. Many on leave, particularly those who were nearing retirement, found jobs in England and did not return, and the suspension of recruitment in 1939 had left the cadres dangerously undermanned.

Indian civil servants and police officers were very worried men; they would have to live in the country after the British had left and this led them to adopt a largely neutral attitude. The new Ministries did little to support them, as they considered them 'lackeys of the British' and allowed local politicians to interfere with the administration at District level. Gone were the days when the District Officer or Superintendent of Police could rely on the support of the Provincial Government. Now the Moslem Officer, who took action against a Hindu or vice versa, might find himself in a very awkward position.

An additional problem arose from the fact that much of the country had become a vast armed camp. The Chief Secretary of the UP gave the following figures of private armies in that Province alone: Congress volunteers 25,000, RSS Sangh — a militant right wing Hindu organisation 25,000, Moslem National Guards 37,000 and Khaksars — an even more militant Moslem force 6,700. There was no shortage of weapons; the demobilisation of large bodies of men, coupled with lax supervision of the disposal of their arms had led to the importation into the Districts of rifles and pistols, together with the appropriate ammunition, on a considerable scale. This was one of my problems in Central Command and it was not helped when the head of the Punjab CID told me that he believed that every type of weapon was hidden in the Province, except a tank, and he could not be absolutely certain that there might not be one of these also. The American Forces were incredibly careless about the disposal of their stores; on one occasion near Agra they threw surplus bombs down disused wells and the improper sales of arms by American personnel reached a high level. The Police, unsupported in many cases by the Provincial Governments were quite unable to make any headway against this threat.

The position in the Armed Forces, by way of contrast, was generally good. The Army was considerably weakened by the progressive withdrawal of British units for demobilisation, but, nevertheless, in both the British units remaining and in the Indian Army, morale remained high and discipline unimpaired. However a nagging fear began to assert itself — it was confidently believed that the Indian soldier would remain loyal in any attempt at rebellion, but how would he react if Hindus and Moslems attacked each other in earnest? Would he be able to resist the temptation to assist his co-religionists, particularly if he had witnessed atrocities committed against them? What would be the position in the 'mixed' units which made up the bulk of the Army?

During this period, I was often out on tour, visiting the various parts of my manor and making contact with the various military HQs, as well as making myself known to the civil and police authorities. This touring was not always pleasant; as most of the Sub Area HQs could only be reached by slow cross country trains; these, however, were often less crowded than the main line mail trains. By May, we were well into the hot weather with temperatures of 115°F, and to make matters worse, I got an attack of boils. This affliction was not uncommon in the hot weather, but the cure, removal to the cool air of a hill station was impossible with the political situation in such a critical state. The poor old horse also succumbed to the heat by getting prickly heat, which caused him to lose his hair on face and neck. The Army Vet could think of no cure, except to tell me not to drive or ride him, but my syce produced an indigenous medicine, 'katila', which cooled the blood. This did the trick but my disobedience of the Vet's instructions made me very unpopular with him.

A number of people in England have commented on the possible dangers prevailing in India at this time, and have thought that at least I was armed when travelling. This was not so; I travelled all over the Command, unarmed and unescorted, except for my Moslem servant, and the worst discomfort I ever suffered was to have had 'Jai Hind' or 'Quit India' shouted at me. The use of these phrases in a derogatory sense sometimes rebounded on the shouter. To shout 'Quit India' at a British soldier usually got the reply 'Wish I blank, blank, could'. General Russell, who officiated for General Scoones, during the latter's absence on leave, was visiting a school when one of the pupils, greatly daring, shouted 'Jai Hind'. The General had the boy brought before him and asked him what he had said; the shivering child replied almost in a whisper 'Jai Hind', at which the General replied in a great bellow 'Jai Hind', adding 'Naturally, I reply with a Jai Hind, since that means victory to India and that is what you and I and everyone wants isn't it?'.

I only made one trip to Nagpur and Kamptee, as there were few problems in the CP. This Province had few Moslems and it was not one which Jinnah would fight about. The Punjab was different and I went to Lahore twice, but the Province remained without any really serious incidents until the autumn, by which time Central Command was no more. I also visited a number of Sub Area HQs, notably Meerut, Amballa and Dehra Dun, but it was to Lucknow that I went most. There were two reasons for this. First, Lucknow was the capital of the UP, a Congress stronghold, and an extremely difficult and turbulent city to control, and second, I found that the Special Superintendent of Police CID (Intelligence), Freddie Stockwell, had married one of my girl friends from pre war days in Dehra Dun. Freddie and Veronica very kindly asked me to stay with them, whenever I was in Lucknow. While I was there I could ride the horses of the Mounted Police and drive Freddie's car, as well as being in an entirely different world to the Army oriented one of Central Command. The war time orders against the wearing of mufti, except for recreation and sport, were still in force. I was authorised to wear mufti, when necessary, but there was little opportunity to do so in Agra. My dinner jacket always went with me to Lucknow and, in the evening, the Stockwells would take me to the United Services Club, housed in the beautiful Chatter Manzil Palace, where I met the senior officers from the UP Secretariat and Police HQ. The first time Freddie lent me his car, I protested that I had no civilian driving licence, as mine had expired when I went overseas in 1941. He said that it did not matter as his orderly would go with me. We had not gone far when we were stopped by a Police Licence check. The orderly and I duly explained that it was Stockwell Sahib's car, but the checking constable refused to let us go, until the matter had been dealt with by his Sahib. I think bad blood between the District Police and the CID was at the bottom of this. We were later released after the arrival of an Inspector.

On one visit to Lucknow serious problems came to the fore. An APM of the British Military Police was shot and killed in broad daylight in the Bazaar, the murderer getting clean away. We were of the opinion that this was the work of the Revolutionary Socialist Party, at that time a terrorist organisation headed by Jai Prakash Narain, then on the run. The next trouble was that the Police reported that the Intelligence Officer of Lucknow Sub Area, a young war time British Officer, was in love with an Indian girl whom the Police suspected of belonging to the same Party. They, naturally, were reluctant to provide him with classified information, so we had to shunt him off to his Regimental Centre, which unfortunately was in the UP and close to Lucknow, put a special censorship on his mail, and recommend that he be posted out of the area as soon as possible. It was symptomatic of the times that while Jai Prakash was on the run, we always knew where he was but a day or two after he had left that location. The Punjab Police finally caught up with him, but he survived to become a Minister in the Janata Ministry not long ago, and a much respected figure.

Not long after my return from Lucknow, a bombshell burst on us at Central Command. It started with a report from the

MIO Bombay that there was likely to be a serious uprising in Lucknow. This had been sent on by MI Branch at Army HQ, who wanted to know why we were ignorant of it. As I was very much in touch with events in Lucknow, I largely discounted this information, but I was probably unwise to say categorically in a Signal that I did not believe half of it, but that I would go to Lucknow to sort matters out. The reply to this was a signal from Pilditch, the Director of the IB to the General — 'Personal for General Scoones from DIB. On no account is Mains to go to Lucknow'. The General's reaction was predictable — he instructed the BGS to signal back to the DMI for the information of Pilditch, that his Chief Intelligence Officer would go where he pleased in his Command. I was reminded of his similar reaction to the criticism of Summersell's arrest of the pair of SOE agents at Manipur Road Base in 1942.

The story gradually emerged: the MIO Bombay, one of the new type, a local British businessman, hastily commissioned and living in his prewar accommodation, got hold of a 'story'. This was by no means uncommon as rumours flew about India on the slightest provocation and there was enough happening in Lucknow to sire any number of them. He then decided to investigate it himself and came to Lucknow without either informing us or his 'masters' in the IB. It was unfortunate that, when he arrived, Freddie Stockwell was away, and he refused to see Mathur the Special Superintendent of Police CID (Crime), who was his stand in, on the quite improper grounds that he, Mathur, was an Indian. He then went to see the District Superintendent of Police, who did not have the overall Intelligence picture and as a result concocted this very alarming report. However the real answer emerged at last. The originator appeared to have been a British Officer, who had been making some very wild statements; the poor fellow had gone off his head, and was awaiting evacuation to Britain as a mental case. The next incident was the murder of Indian soldiers in Lucknow; this the Police traced to a gang of Pathans, who were hanging about the Indian Armoured Corps Depot with the intention of robbing soldiers of their demobilisation money. The case of the Intelligence Officer of Lucknow Sub Area we knew about, and had taken appropriate action, but the most interesting incident was the murder of the APM; the full facts of which did not emerge until the following year.

I had heard on one of my visits to Lucknow, that a British soldier, Sapper Hart had deserted from the RTO's office at Lucknow Station. This was not of great moment, as desertion was a disciplinary matter dealt with by AG's Branch, and anyway, a British deserter usually gave himself up or was arrested pretty quickly. The fact that he had absconded with a rifle was never reported and this was of importance both to Army Intelligence and the Police. It was established afterwards that it was he who had shot the APM. Hart later joined, and is thought to have led, a very active band of dacoits, who were operating in the difficult country on the borders of the UP and Gwalior State. He was finally caught by the Police, and charged with murder. It was regrettable that, as Indian Independence was only a few months away, he was not claimed for trial by Court Martial but was allowed to stand trial in the Lucknow Sessions Court. What was doubly unfortunate was that as a European he could claim trial by a jury of 'Europeans and Americans' instead of the usual trial by a Judge assisted by two Assessors. This provision for cases of murder, and one or two other serious crimes, had been written into the Criminal Procedure Code in the eighteen eighties, at the time when Europeans were made subject to trial by Indian Judges. The result was that he was acquitted of Murder and only received two years Rigorous Imprisonment for illegal possession of arms. Two facts were detrimental to this case — the first was the neglect of reporting the theft of a rifle to the Intelligence Branch and the Police; the other was that Hart was known as a dangerous criminal in England, and there was a strong suspicion that the British Police had quietly steered him towards the Army as a way of getting rid of him; and even worse his dossier had never been given to the Army or sent to India. This was in marked contrast to the liaison between the Police and Army in case of communists and fellow travellers; we had a comprehensive knowledge of the whereabouts of these, as a result of information from the British Police and Intelligence Agencies.

On the political front the question was — what would Jinnah do now? That we were in for a period of very serious communal violence was obvious, but where and how was as yet uncertain. Our appreciation was that there would be violence in most of the major cities, but that in the Centre and South this was only likely in such industrial centres as Bombay and Ahmadabad. These outbreaks, although likely to be serious, were unlikely to make the British Government change its mind about the establishment of Pakistan. There were two points where Jinnah would have to make a major impact — one was Bengal, where he would have to convince the Government that, if the whole of this Moslem majority Province and, in particular Calcutta could not be included in Pakistan, then no one else would be able to rule it; the other was the Punjab, here Jinnah regarded a Congress ministry ruling a Moslem majority Province as a running sore which must be excised.

The campaign was started by the Moslem League committee on the 29th July by reversing their acceptance of the Cabinet Mission Plan and stating publically that they were prepared to resort to 'Direct Action' to achieve their aims. They then nominated the 16th of August as 'Direct Action Day' and ordered a complete hartal of Moslem businesses and shops coupled with meetings, processions and demonstrations. That there would be trouble on that day was obvious, but we were fortunate that in our flash points, the UP and our part of the Punjab, the scale of violence was comparatively low. Troops were put on the alert, in cities such as Lucknow and Lahore as a precautionary measure, but were not needed; the Police were able to deal with any trouble that occurred.

The Moslem League Government in Bengal provoked trouble by an act of incredible folly; they declared Direct Action Day a public holiday. This was a formula for violence, particularly in Calcutta, where the Moslems were in a minority. The Ministry was warned by the leader of the Congress Party in the Bengal Assembly that the Hindus would not observe the Hartal and would meet force with force if there was any attempt to coerce them. The Sikhs, not to be outdone, declared that if the Moslems wanted trouble they were going the right way to get it. The Day started peacefully enough with Moslem processions converging on central Calcutta for a mammoth meeting to be addressed by the Chief Minister, Mr. Suhrawady, but before long the Hindus started to erect barricades to impede the Moslem marchers. The Police still hoped the day would pass off with only minor incidents. No one knows who actually started the violence, but by mid afternoon reports were received of communal attacks all over north Calcutta, and by evening control had been lost and the troops were called out.

This violence followed a different pattern to the previous anti Government riots, and it was one that was far more difficult to control. Previously the mobs had attacked Government buildings, police stations, large shops and business premises, mainly situated on main highways, so that the troops were able to move in quickly to disperse them. Now, although it was still possible to control the major highways, troops could do little good in the crowded slum areas of north Calcutta. Here the two communities fought each other with appalling savagery, using iron bars, swords and spears as well as firearms. Large areas of slum property were set alight, and as the Fire Brigade were unable to reach, much less to contain, these outbreaks, all within were burnt to death. The outbreak spread to the normally peaceful area of south Calcutta on the next day and the holocaust continued unabated until the night of the 18th August, when the Calcutta garrison, now comprising eight battalions, four British and four Indian or Gurkha, made a supreme effort and finally gained control of north Calcutta. Slowly confidence returned to the city but it was several days before the corpses were removed, the streets tidied up, and essential services restored. The sweepers, the only caste prepared to handle dead bodies, had either fled or been slaughtered, so the brunt of this horrific and herculean task fell on the British soldiers, who on one night alone removed four hundred corpses, many in a state of decay. It was estimated that 6,000 died and 20,000 were injured to say nothing of the many thousands rendered homeless.

The communities now started a game of 'tit for tat'. The arrival in Chittagong of Moslem refugees from Calcutta sparked off a serious riot, and later, in October, the Moslem majority in Eastern Bengal started a dress rehearsal for Pakistan by a campaign of harrassment and forced conversions, designed to drive out the Hindus. It required a Brigade of troops to restore the situation; the behaviour of the troops was exemplary and their impartiality without question, but the fact that the Commander was a Hindu Brigadier caused widespread condemnation by the Moslems. The situation was helped by the sturdy commonsense of the Governor, Sir Frederick Burrows, ex Guards Sergeant Major and ex official of the National Union of Railwaymen, and also by Gandhi, who went to Noakhali District vowing that he would either bring peace or leave his bones there. He was helpful and moderate, unlike his previous behaviour and his presence at this time did much to keep Bengal peaceful at Independence, a year later.

The trouble in East Bengal was the last of which I had official cognizance, as Central Command was being abolished and divided between Eastern and Northern Commands. However to continue the tit for tat story; it was not long after the Bengal trouble that the Hindus in Bihar rose and slaughtered every Moslem that they could get their hands on. The UP continued to rumble on with sporadic attacks until a very violent outbreak occurred at a fair on the banks of the Ganges in Meerut District, which spread over the adjoining country side. Finally in the early part of 1947, the long awaited attack by the Moslem League aimed at bringing down the Congress Government in the Punjab broke out. After about a month of anarchy, the Governor dismissed the Ministry and took over the government himself. These were only the major outbreaks, violence could, and did, break out without warning from time to time all over northern India.

There were sporadic outbreaks in Agra from Direct Action Day onward, but we were fortunate in having two first rate civil officers; Hubert Evans, the District Magistrate, and Wood, the Superintendent of Police, both highly regarded and respected by all. They realised that all too often, a violent outbreak stemmed from a very minor incident, which if dealt with immediately stopped further violence, so posses of Police in tents were stationed at important points in the City ready to deal with anyone likely to cause a breach of the peace.

Communalism was beginning to show itself everywhere; even Officer's servants were not immune and we began to have squabbles between them when waiting on their Masters at meal times in the Mess. I was told that the Mess barman, late at night, boasted to young British Officers of what he would do to the Hindus, when the Moslem National Guards took over Agra, and produced a green uniform from under the Bar. I decided that enough was enough and interviewed him without delay; I told him bluntly that if I had another word out of him, I would have him taken to the Police Station and get the Station House Officer to give him a beating that he would not forget in a hurry. This did the trick and there was no further trouble.

CHAPTER TEN

The Winding Up of Central Command — Marriage — The End of my Time in Intelligence

Cᴇɴᴛʀᴀʟ Command was going to be partitioned between Eastern and Northern Commands on 1st October and we were now in August, so I felt that it was time that my future was clarified. The year before I had been recommended for the six months Staff College Course starting in midsummer 1946, but Army HQ had sent this back with a rider that I would receive more benefit from the first of the post war one year Courses starting in January 1947. I approached the BGS to get the General's backing for this; I had learnt that, Pauline, my wife, to be, was likely to get an air passage and arrive at the end of September, when we would be married, so I suggested hopefully that I might be given leave after the wind up of the Command. The General did me proud by giving me the strongest possible recommendation, and also, two months leave, with a letter to the Military Secretary's Branch that 'this Officer will be available for reposting on the expiry of his leave'.

The Major General Administration was not satisfied with the financial administration of the three Officers' Messes. The pre war system of grants, subscriptions, and payments, was extremely complicated, and during the war audit control was largely relaxed, but now had been re-established. By custom

the post of PMC, President of the Mess Committee, went to
the senior of the Officers in mess; this resulted in specialist
Officers such as the Command Catering or Local Resources
Officers, or the Deputy Judge Advocate holding these posts as
they were Temporary Colonels, but as they were war time
commissioned, they had scant knowledge of pre war procedure.
The result was that Officers in the past had not been charged
for such items as electricity, hire of furniture and such like,
and the Military Accounts Department was now presenting the
Messes with large bills. It would be very unfair to charge the
present Officers for sums incurred before ever they had entered
the Mess and the others had in many cases left India on
demobilisation.

The MGA's solution was to issue orders that Officers must
be charged forthwith for these items on their monthly Mess
Bills, and that the senior *Regular Officer* would take over the
duties of PMC, investigate the debts and report the Mess's
indebtedness. I was the senior Regular in 'B' Mess so I got the
job; it involved a lot of work getting Courts of Enquiry
convened, and later, putting up cases for the various amounts
to be written off. A welcome break from this job was a visit
to Army HQ for a one day conference of Senior Intelligence
Officers which was to be addressed by the Director of Military
Intelligence, General Cawthorne. I had expected that he would
expound on the situation in India, but, on the contrary, he
explained the post war aims of Russia. Most of us had thought
that we were all friends and allies, and that we were in for
some years of peace. The DMI disillusioned us by stating the
exact opposite; Russia it appeared was determined that the next
war would not be fought on her soil, so she would not rest
until she had a ring of friendly states around her borders, and
would use force, if necessary, to obtain this.

A visit also from a Colonel Grant-Taylor, an expert in the
use of the pistol, was another welcome break from routine.
Grant-Taylor had started his career as a European constable in
the Shanghai police, where he came to the conclusion that the
Police with their cumbersome holsters and method of taking
aim, did not stand a chance against the armed criminal. The

method he devised caught on in the USA where as I understand it, he was pistol Instructor to both the FBI and the Chicago Police Department. He returned to England during the war, and was employed as pistol Instructor to the Commandos, and now he had been sent to explain his methods to the Indian Army. What he taught was completely at variance with the Army's standard methods, involving two handed rested shooting when this was possible, the abolition of the use of double action, and its replacement by cocking the pistol with the thumb, and, most revolutionary of all, holding the weapon so that the index finger pointed at the target and firing without using the sights, on the same principle as a shot gun is aimed. Most of these methods are now standard practice in the SAS and the Police. The General was extremely interested and suggested that Bill Moorshead and I familiarised ourselves with Grant-Taylor's teaching. I must confess that with the old methods I was the world's worst shot, but I now became an excellent one. The General ordered that a competition should be held between our HQ, and the local British Tank Regiment and Infantry Battalion. We all took this very seriously; Bill and I could be seen walking about the HQ cocking and snapping an empty revolver to obtain the necessary speed in firing. The two other units picked teams of young subalterns and struck them off all other duties. Our team was somewhat elderly in comparison, Bill Moorshead, who was about forty, myself, who was nearly thirty four, and an elderly Sikh Captain from the Lands and Cantonements Branch. The competition included two handed long distance shooting and 'shooting up a room', five targets to be engaged in a very short period of time. We won much to the delight of the General, and I still have the Tankard, which he presented to me.

The BGS decided that we should have a 'winding up' party for the staff of General Staff Branch. He arranged that we should take over 'A' Mess, which was the nearest to our offices, for a tea party which would be attended by not only Officers and Clerks, but also our Chaprassis who would have curry and rum in a tent in the garden. I drove down in the trap and told my chaprassi to look after my syce. Later the BGS, accompanied by the section Heads went out to see how they were enjoying themselves, and there was the horse, tethered to a guy rope looking into the tent with a most debauched look. I asked the syce on the way home if it had been a good 'khana' and got the reply 'Hic! very good khana, Sahib — Hic! very good khana' The old man had had a really good go at the rum.

I received a cable from Pauline saying that she had got her passage and was likely to arrive shortly after the 20th September, so I now had to get busy in arranging her arrival and our wedding. I had to approach the BGS for leave to go to Delhi to meet her, give the required notice to the District Magistrate, who was also the Registrar of Civil Marriages, book a room at the Cecil Hotel in Agra for us to live in, and what was more difficult get a Hotel room in Delhi 'on tap', should the plane be delayed and I had to stay there. Hotel rooms in Delhi were almost impossible to obtain, but, luckily, Peter Cane, the CO of our Fourth Battalion, which was stationed in Delhi, had influence through his father in law, so all was well.

The Flight was late, so I had to ring the Office daily to ask Bill Moorshead if the BGS would allow me to remain. Agra was experiencing one of its periodic riots, and this was to cause a slight upset in Headquarters. I was lunching with Alfred Wagg, an American War Correspondent, who had been with us on the early part of the Burma Retreat and, later, had visited Burma Army HQ at Tamu when we were on our way out. 'Waggie' was very pro British, but was one of those people who often give the wrong impression; at this time he was a Special Correspondent of the 'National Call', one of the most anti British of the English language dailies. During lunch I was called to the telephone to speak to Bill Moorshead about the extension to my leave and, in the course of the conversation, I asked him about 'his riot' and got the latest casualty figures, which were quite light — about five or six killed. I mentioned them to Waggie, who asked if he could use them and as there was nothing secret about it, I agreed. The following day, all the papers referred to the Agra riot, and like newspapers, then and now, all had different figures for the casualties; the only correct one was in the National Call. While there was no security breach, this upset Bill Moorshead, who wondered who in the HQ was in touch with such an anti British paper. There was a good deal of merriment, when it transpired that the figures had been given by the Chief Intelligence Officer himself. The great day arrived at last and, on the afternoon of the 26th September, my wife to be stepped off the plane at Delhi Airport. It was too late to go on to Agra that day, so we stayed the night in Delhi and went on by train on the following day arriving in Agra in time for dinner. What followed was the reverse of romantic, as after dinner I left Pauline in the Hotel telling her that I would not see her until 3 p.m. on the following day, when I would come in a car to take her to the Collectorate for the wedding.

The next morning, I went to the Office to take up my duties again; luckily I asked Bill, when he went down to the City Police Station, to remind Hubert Evans that he was marrying us at 3 p.m., just in case the riot had put it out of his mind; which indeed it had. Our witnesses were Bill and Hurst, my GSO III I(a), with Mrs. Moorshead also present. I thought that we should at least have a wedding photograph for our families, but this was something of an initiation to India for Pauline, as while the photographer was setting up his old fashioned apparatus, Bill and Hubert were having an animated discussion about the latest riot casualties. Remarks like 'I think it was six killed' — 'No it was seven, you have not counted the chap in the sack' — 'Yes, I have but what about the one in the drain'.

We naturally wished to have a Wedding Reception, but the difficulty was to fix the date; on the day of our wedding the RAF Group were having a farewell party at Agra Airfield, and all those whom we would have wished to invite were going there, the following day was a Sunday, and on Monday the Deputy Military Secretary was having his farewell party, but luckily he agreed to postpone this until Tuesday, as he did not think that the Ham that had been ordered from the Army and Navy Stores in Bombay would arrive in time. We had a first class party in 'B' Mess, with everyone from the General and the BGS down; eventually we collected the stragglers and adjourned to the local Chinese Restaurant for dinner; a very hilarious meal.

This Monday was the 30th September, the last day before command passed to Northern and Eastern Commands, and I had my last Intelligence Summary to write. My civilian police stenographer was caught up in the curfew imposed in the City and could not get to Office. Pauline, however, had been employed in London as Personal Assistant to the GSO I of the Australian HQ there; she knew the form and the military jargon, so I suggested to the BGS that she should be co-opted to take down and type the Summary, and this gave her the entry to the winding up beer party which he gave to the Officers and Clerks of the Branch.

However before we could start our honeymoon in Kashmir, we still had a week's work to do winding up 'B' Mess. During this time, I was able to show Pauline something of the wonderful Mogul buildings in Agra and to dispel any ideas that she may have had of the hatred of the Indians for the British. She was enchanted with all she saw and by the friendly and courteous behaviour of the average Indian. A day or so after our marriage, she wanted to go to the Bazaar in the pony trap; I could not go with her, but I assured her that while the syce would look after her, she would have to drive as it would be a great loss of face, if he drove her. She set off in some trepidation, which was not eased when she arrived at the main cross roads in the Bazaar, with the usual throng milling about. Putting a brave face on it she rang the trap's warning bell, at which the traffic policeman looked up, saw it was my trap, blew a blast on his whistle to warn the populace, waved her on and as she went by came smartly to attention and saluted.

We set off for Kashmir on the 7th of October, thus ending my career in Security Intelligence.

Epilogue

ALTHOUGH I was never employed again in Intelligence, I continued to serve in India until January 1953, when owing to Independence I was retired.

Pauline and I had a wonderful honeymoon in Kashmir on our two months leave. Our Houseboat was moored on Nagin Bagh few miles out of Srinagar. The season had just ended so we had the place almost to ourselves and the sole use of a small yacht. The water was too cold to bathe, but we could sun ourselves in the glorious autumn sunshine; later when the evenings grew cold, the boat owner produced a stove for our living room, so we were very comfortable.

The question on our return to Agra in early December, was what job I would be given. I found that I was on the list of those who would join the Staff College at Quetta in mid February, two and a half months away. In the ordinary course of events, I should have gone to our Regimental Centre at Dehra Dun, but this would have the inconvenience of a double move, together with the difficulty of finding married quarters, while in Agra we could live in comfort in the Cecil Hotel. As a War Substantive Major, I should not lose rank whatever job I had so I persuaded the Brigade Major of Agra Sub Area to take me into the Sub Area HQ as an Attaché General Staff.

We arrived in Quetta without mishap, together with the horse and trap. The Course had an unusual collection of students, in fact, most of the British Students were senior to the Indian Directing Staff, and often to the British Staff as well. The reason was that many of them could not, or had not, done the course earlier; in my case because I had got on well enough in Intelligence without it, and others had been Prisoners of War and this was their first opportunity. Thus, it was possible to find a student who had been at practically every operation that the British Forces had taken part in. We even had an Officer who had commanded the hush hush force that had broken into King Farouk's Palace, and held him prisoner until he promised to dismiss his pro Axis Ministry in favour of one who favoured the Allies.

The situation in the Punjab and adjacent territories was going from bad to worse, and the arrival of Mountbatten, as Viceroy, with his proposal to partition the country and grant Independence by the 15th of August caused great dismay. However much of this went over our heads; we had plenty of work, with excellent facilities for sport of every sort. I acquired a second horse and set about teaching Pauline to ride. There was no trouble in Quetta, until about a fortnight after Independence, and although this involved a massacre of Hindus and Sikhs in outlying Districts, order was quickly restored. Nevertheless what did concern us all was the future both of the Course and of the British Officers of the Indian Army. The Course was declared 'neutral' and was to have continued until December, but the two Dominions, at each other's throats in Kashmir, demanded their Officers back, so the last two months instruction had to be concertined to allow a closure in mid October. The British Officers of the Indian Army were given three options — to retire with compensation for loss of career, to transfer to the British Army, or, for a limited number, to serve for a limited period in the Army of either India or Pakistan, forfeiting the option of transfer to the British Army, but receiving the compensation. The conditions for transfer, as laid down by the Chief of the Imperial General Staff, Field Marshal Montgomery, meant that I could not continue to serve either in Gurkhas or in British Infantry, but would have to become a 'Gunner', and mathematics had always been a closed book to me. We decided, therefore, to opt for continued service in the Indian Army.

I was accepted and ordered to move to our Regimental Centre at Dehra Dun on the conclusion of the course, while the authorities made up their minds as to how I should be employed. The problem was how to get there. Very shortly after Independence, the Government of Pakistan stated that rail travel between the Dominions was unsafe owing to attacks on trains, and a day or so later the Railway Administration suspended all scheduled services across, and in the vicinity, of the border. We should have had to travel as far as Lahore by such ordinary trains as were still running, and try and get a place on a troop special onwards. This had grave disadvantages, first, if not actually dangerous, travel would be very uncomfortable, and second the railway could not guarantee the safe conveyance of luggage. As we had several packing cases of household goods, which could not be stowed in our carriage, it looked as if we should lose them. Another Staff College student went by this way and lost all his booked luggage, besides having to stand guard over his compartment to prevent locals, for whom there was no place on the overcrowded train, breaking in.

There was another option — to travel on the special that was taking the Indian Staff and student Officers back to India, together with India's allocation of the College's staff and assets. This train was booked to go to Delhi, from whence, it was possible to travel by ordinary services. I asked the acting Commandant for his permission and was told bluntly, that I was a fool and we should surely be murdered on route. I did not think, however, that this train would be attacked as it would have a very strong escort, but I was certain that if we went by any other route, we would lose all our household kit. He then washed his hands of us and agreed. The next thing was to find a way to get my two horses and the trap away; luck was on our side, the Indian AA & QMG of the Airborne Division was paying for a horsebox to be attached to their train which was going straight through to Dehra, and was overjoyed to find someone who would share the cost.

The next problem was to make arrangements for our servants; the two Hindu syces would go with the horses and the sweeper would come on our train with the Staff College menials.

The cook and the waiter were Moslem locals, but with great reluctance, I felt that I could not take the responsibility of taking my Moslem bearer across the disturbed areas. This was a wrench for me as I had had him since I was a 2/Lieutenant, and he had only recently rejoined me after wartime separation. We found that a British couple, who were returning to England, had two Hindu servants, a Gurkha bearer and a Magh cook, so we did a swap; they took my three Moslems to serve them until they were allotted a passage, and I took their two Hindus back to India. The Gurkha had to be sent back to Nepal for health reasons in 1950, but the cook remained with us until we left India in 1953, and a wonderful cook he was.

The Officer's accommodation on the train was not very comfortable; there was one ordinary I & II Class carriage and two 'Military Car Officers'. The few berths in the ordinary carriage would be taken by the senior Instructors and their families, the rest of us were to travel in the Military Cars, which were a slightly more comfortable version of the vehicles allocated before the war to British soldiers — couchette type compartments with scanty lavatory accommodation and little privacy. We were lucky that the most senior Indian Officer, Brigadier Verma, had gone ahead by air leaving his wife and small son to follow by train. He told her, for her safety, not to travel alone in a two berth compartment but in a four berth with another married couple; she chose Pauline and I so we travelled in comparative comfort in a I Class four berth compartment — four humans and three dogs.

We had been allotted as escort two Sikh companies of the Frontier Force Regiment, returning to India, and it was nice to know that their Moslem compatriots mounted a road escort through the Bolan Pass, where the road and railway run side by side. The descent of the Pass was nearly our undoing, as the brake power was insufficient for a train of fourteen coaches on a 1 in 40 gradient and the driver had great difficulty in getting the load under control. It was discovered that several of the coaches had defective brakes, although they had been passed as fit to run by the Train Examiner at Quetta. Whether this was a deliberate act of sabotage, or merely the desire of the Pakistan authorities to send only the oldest and most decrepit stock on cross border trains, will never be known.

The journey otherwise was uneventful and not uncomfortable for us, except that we were 24 hours late in arriving at Amballa, to which destination we had been diverted owing to Delhi being isolated by floods. We landed on our feet again as we found my old Battalion, the 2nd, was stationed there. The Battalion was a post war reconstitution of the 5th Battalion, and contained many Officers and men who were my friends. Through their good offices, we were able in due course to get a lift in a lorry going to Dehra.

We remained in The Regimental Centre until January 1948, while the powers that be were making up their minds as to how I should be employed. The Centre was in some confusion; the Commandant, Colonel Robinson, was still British, although he was expecting to be ordered off for repatriation at any minute; a few Indian Officers had already been posted in to replace the outgoing British; these were mostly ethnic Gurkhas, who were Indian subjects, and up to now precluded from serving in Gurkha Regiments. Colonel Robinson's first remark to me was 'You have no business to be here', and he produced an AG Branch letter showing the names of Officers who were under posting to the Centre. I countered this with a copy of an MS Branch order definitely posting me in. The trouble was that 'AO' Robinson, a friend of long standing, was uncertain as to how to employ me, and more important, where he was going to find a married quarter in the overcrowded lines. However both these matters were resolved; I was given command of HQ Company and we managed to obtain a small three roomed bungalow, which luckily had a cookhouse. The horses and the trap duly turned up and we settled to two wonderful months in probably one of the most beautiful stations in India and in the glorious winter weather.

We had one disappointment, when after having being short-listed, I failed to get the appointment of First Secretary of the British Embassy in Nepal but subsequently I was appointed, by India, Commandant of our Regimental Centre with the rank of Lieutenant Colonel. Before I had had time to take over, the authorities changed their minds as to the desirability of having a British Officer in such a post; this seemed a blow as we would have much enjoyed continuing our stay in Dehra, but, in fact, was a blessing in disguise as I would have had only a year in this appointment.

The final offer was that of Chief Staff Officer (GSO I) of the Infantry School at Mhow in Central India. The problem now was, how to get the horses and trap there; passenger train services were now nearly normal, but it would be very difficult for me to obtain a horse box. I then thought of the Choudhri, the Regimental Contractor, and asked him to come and see me. I told him that I was leaving behind two horses and two men, would he please ration them until departure; further would he obtain a horse box from the railway, load the horses, trap and syces, ration them for the journey and book the horse box to Mhow including a second box due to a break of gauge, and finally send me a bill. All he replied was 'very good, Sahib', and he was as good as his word.

Mhow was a very lovely place, situated in the old State of Indore, with an excellent climate. India kept us for five years and I can say honestly that these were some of the best years of my service. When I finally retired in January 1953, I joined the British Regular Army Reserve of Officers in the Intelligence Corps, but I was never called up, so my service in Intelligence ended with the closure of Central Command; it had been an interesting time as I was in at the very beginning and can call myself the 'Father' of the Indian Field Security Service.

THE CIVIL, MILITARY, AND POLICE ORGANISATION IN INDIA

The Civil Government

General

It might be said that, in 1939 the British 'ruled' India, but did not govern it; the governing was done by the Indians themselves on behalf of the British. The number of superior civil servants, the Indian Civil Service, was only about one thousand of which half were Indians. There were no British personnel among the thousands of lesser civil servants, magistrates and revenue officers. India was divided into British India, the Native States and Tribal Territory.

British India

British India was divided into semi autonomous Provinces, each with a Governor, and a Ministry responsible to the Provincial Legislature. The Governor had the power, with the concurrence of the Viceroy, to take over the Government and rule directly if this became necessary. The Provinces were divided into Districts, each ruled by a District Magistrate, not unlike a French Prefet. The Central Government was headed by the Viceroy and Governor General, assisted by a Council, which was the equivalent to a Cabinet, except that its members were neither members of, nor responsible to, the Central Legislature.

The Native States

There were some three hundred States of varying size and standards of administration, but only about twenty were of any considerable area or importance. They all had Treaties with the British Crown, and, except in foreign relations, were technically independent. To keep the rulers in order and to ensure some standard of administration, the doctrine of Paramountcy had been evolved. This meant that any advice tendered officially by the Government of India was Paramount and must be acted upon.

Tribal Territory

The inhabitatnts of the tribal territories in the North West and North East were allowed to go their own ways, provided they behaved themselves and did not raid into administered territory.

Military Organisation

The Army in India

This term was used to cover all the land forces of the Crown in India, irrespective of whether they belonged to the British Army (usually known as the British Service) or the Indian Army. The Army in India was autonomous, both for operational purposes and administration, subject to the overall control of the British Parliament, through the Secretary of State for India.

The British Service

This comprised a number of Cavalry, Infantry and Artillery units stationed in India. These units, while remaining a part of the British Army, were, during their service in India, not only operationally commanded, but, also, administered, equipped and paid by India. It might be said that they were 'on loan', and thus differed from British units serving in other parts of the British Empire who remained under the control of the British War Office. The British units were dependent on the Indian Army for their supporting arms, except Artillery, and administrative services.

The Indian Army

The Indian Army consisted, in general, of Indian soldiers and British Officers but it was beginning to have a sizeable number of Indian Officers. It was self contained except for Horse and Field Artillery, which, since 1861 had been provided by units of the British Royal Artillery. It was usual, however, to have one British Cavalry Regiment or Infantry Battalion in each Indian Cavalry or Infantry Brigade. There were no British Warrant Officers or NCOs in Indian Cavalry of Infantry units. The only Artillery in the Indian Army, with the exception of the newly raised 1st Indian Field Regiment was unbrigaded Mountain Batteries, normally allocated to the North West Frontier. Engineer and Signal units were provided by the Indian Army, consisting of British Officers seconded from the Royal Engineers or Royal Corps of Signals and Indian soldiers. As a result of Indianisation, there were now Indian Officers in the 1st Field Regiment and Engineer and Signals units commissioned direct into these Corps. The administrative services were provided by the Indian Army Service Corps and the Indian Army Ordnance Corps; no units of the Royal Army Service Corps nor Royal Army Ordnance Corps served in India.

The Indian Army differed from the British Army in that commissioned Officers did not serve below Company Second in Command. Platoons were commanded by officers promoted from the ranks; they held commissions from the Viceroy and not from the Sovereign, and were junior to 2nd Lieutenants. The ranks were Jemadar (one star), Subedar (two stars) and Subedar Major (a crown); they had no equivalent in the British Army. The non commissioned ranks had separate designations:

Lance Naik	Lance Corporal
Naik	Corporal
Havildar	Sergeant

The above refer to Infantry; the cavalry had the same rank structure, but with different designations. Daffadar = Havildar, Lance Daffadar = Naik.

Police Organisation

The Police were Government servants and the Provincial Inspector General was responsible to the Provincial Government for the administration of his force but had no executive functions. The executive officer was the Superintendent, who commanded the Police in his District, subject to the overall control of the District Magistrate. The poor educational standards of the Constable meant that he was only used for beat work, crowd and traffic control. This led to a three tier structure of Gazetted Officers, Subordinate Officers and Constables. A Gazetted Officer entered direct as an Assistant Superintendent after a civil service examination; the gazetted ranks were Assistant, and Deputy Superintendent, Superintendent, Deputy Inspector General and Inspector General. Subordinate Officers entered as Sub Inspectors, with promotion to Inspector. Sergeants, ranking between Sub Inspectors and Inspectors were recruited from Anglo Indians or time expired British soldiers. Constables could normally expect promotion to Naik and Head Constable (Havildar).

The major cities of Calcutta, Madras, Bombay and Rangoon had separate police departments directly under the Home Department of the Provincial Government and not under the Inspector General. The gazetted officers were seconded from the provincial force and held the ranks of Assistant and Deputy Commissioner and Commissioner.

Glossary

Indian Government, Military and Police — Terms and abbreviations

AA	Anti Aircraft
AA & QMG	Assistant Adjutant and Quartermaster General — A senior Administrative Staff Officer
A or AG	Adjutant General's Branch
AT	Animal Transport
AILO	Air Intelligence Liason Officer
ALFSEA	Allied Land Forces, South East Asia
BATS	Code name for Indian soldiers dropped by parachute in Assam to spy for the Japanese
BGS	Brigadier, General Staff
BurCorps	Burma Corps comprising 17 Ind Div and 1 BurDiv
BurDiv	Burma Division
CID	Criminal Investigation Department
CO	Commanding Officer
CRP	Crown Representative's Police
DIB	Director, Intelligence Bureau (Government of India)
DME	District Mechanical Engineer (Railways)
DTS	District Traffic Superintendent (Railways)
EA Div	East African Division
FAL	Frontier Armoured Lorry
FS	Field Security
FSO	Field Security Officer

FSP	Field Security Police
FSS	Field Security Service
GOC	General Officer Commanding (Division or Area)
GOC in C	General Officer Commanding in Chief (Corps or Army)
GS	General Staff Branch
GS I	General Staff — Intelligence (See also 'Intelligence')
GS Ops	General Staff — Operations
GS Trg	General Staff — Training
GS SD	General Staff — Staff Duties
GSO I	General Staff Officer 1st Grade (Lieutenant Colonel)
GSO II	General Staff Officer 2nd Grade (Major)
GSO III	General Staff Officer 3rd Grade (Captain)
HQ	Headquarters
I	Intelligence Section of the General Staff, divided into:
	I(a) Operational Intelligence
	I(b) Security Intelligence
	I(c) Public Relations and Censorship, later abolished
	I(d) Deception
	I(x) Administration
IB	Intelligence Bureau, Govt of India
ICS	Indian Civil Service
INA	Indian National Army (see also 'JIFS').
Ind Div	Indian Division.
JIFs	Japanese Inspired Forces (later INA). Indian soldiers who defected to the Japanese.
L of C	Lines of Communication.
MES	Military Engineering Service
MIO	Military Intelligence Officer, Military Officer seconded to the Intelligence Bureau.
MGA	Major General, Administration.
MO	Medical Officer
MP	Military Police(man)

MT	Mechanical Transport
NCO	Non Commissioned Officer
OR	Other Rank
PA	Political Agent
PM	Punjabi Mussulman, Moslem community in the Punjab, much enlisted
PWD	Public Works Department (of civil Government)
QM	Quartermaster
Q or QMG	Quartermaster General's Branch.
RIAF	Royal Indian Air Force
RIN	Royal Indian Navy
2i/c	Second in Command
SEAC	South East Asia Command
SIB	Special Investigation Branch (Military Police)
SP	Superintendent of Police
VCO	Viceroys Commissioned Officer (See Appx A)
V Force	Para Military Force operating on Indo-Burma frontier to combat infiltrators
WAC(I)	Womens Auxiliary Corps (India)
WA Div	West African Division
WO	Warrant Officer
Z Force	Intelligence Organisation raised to gather information behind the Japanese lines in Burma

Indian and other non British terms

Babu	Clerk
Cantonements	Military area of Indian town
Chaprassi	Official messenger
Charpoy	Indian type bedstead
Civil Lines	European area of Indian town
Dacoits	Bandits
Goondas	Urban gangsters
HH	His Highness (Indian ruling Prince)
ITA	Indian Tea Association
Khana	Food, Dinner
Kutchery	District Magistrate's Offices and Courts

Lathis	Staves used by Indian Police
Magh	Arakanese Buddhist domiciled in India in Chittagong District; provided some of the best European style cooks
Mahout	Elephant driver
Posteen	Sheepskin coat
Scheduled } Castes	Untouchables, so called as they were specified in a 'schedule' of the Government of India Act
Serang	Native Captain of a river steamer
Shikari	Sportsman
Souk	Middle East equivalent to the Indian 'Bazaar'
Syce	Groom
Sweeper	Untouchable who deals with night soil and latrines
Tonga	Indian two wheeled horse vehicle plying for hire
WL	Wagon Lit (International Sleeping car Company)

LIEUTENANT COLONEL A. A. MAINS

9th Gurkha Rifles, Indian Army

1932–33	Royal Military College — Prize Cadet, Cadet Scholarship, Modern History Prize.
1934	Commissioned into Unattached List Indian Army — att 1 Dorsets in India.
1935	Joined 2/9th Gurkha Rifles. Regimental duty until Jan 1941.
Mar 1939	Command Intelligence Course — Passed out 1st. Recommended for Indian Political Intelligence.
Aug 1939	Offered appointment as 'Military Intelligence Officer' Eastern States, Ranchi. Secondment to Civil Police with rank of Additional Superintendent of Police. Vetoed by CO owing to shortage of Officers on outbreak of War.
Jan 1941	Instructor Class 'C' at new Indian Intelligence School.
Apr 41–Jan 42	Chief Security Officer, Iraq Force, Bagdad (GSO III).
Jan 42–May 42	BURMA RETREAT. Chief Security Officer, Burma Army. (GSO II). Asst Military Governor, Law & Order, Rangoon, during evacuation.
Jan 42–Jan 43	Chief Security Officer, Assam, (GSO II. 4 Corps & OC Gauhati Intelligence Detachment).
Jan 43–Oct 43	Chief Intelligence Officer, Assam, (GSO II, 202 L of C Area)
Oct 43–Sep 44	Chief Security Officer, XIV Army (GSO II).

Sep 44–Mar 46	2 i/c 5/9th Gurkha Rifles, Baluchistan & NW Frontier.
Mar 46–Sep 46	Chief Intelligence Officer, Central Command, India (GSO I).
1947	Student Staff College, Quetta, awarded 'psc'.
	After short period at Regimental Centre during hand over to Indian Officers:
Jan 48–Dec 52	Chief Staff Officer, Indian Infantry School, Mhow after Independence

After retirement

1970–82	Member, Indian Services Committee, National Army Museum
1975–85	Member, Executive Committee later Trustee, Gurkha Museum.
1976–86	Chairman, Indian Army Association
Currently	Member, Society for Army Historical Research. Member, Military Historical Society. Hon Member, Indian Military Collectors Society (Toronto). Consultant Historian to the Gurkha Museum.

Writings, broadcasting etc.

Books	'Retreat from Burma — An Intelligence Officer's Personal Story', W. Foulsham & Co Ltd, Slough, 1973, Paperback following year.
	Unpublished — 'Sorrowful Departure', History of Indian Independence.
	'Railways of the Raj'.

Major Articles

(a) Railway Gazette —
      'Journey from Pakistan to India 1947'.

(b) Army Quarterly —
October 1971 — 'Pakistan — What went wrong'. April 1972 — 'India & Pakistan — What now?

(c) Fodors
(i) 'Railways of the World' Editorial Contributor on Indian Railways.
(ii) 1974 India Guide — section on railway travel.

(d) Journal of the Society of Army Historical Research.
(i) 'The Auxiliary Force (India)' — Autumn 1982.
(ii) 'The Organisation of Indian Infantry 1903–39' — Autumn 1986.

(e) The Bulletin (Journal of the Military Historical Society). 'Indian Soldiers serving in British Units' — Autumn 1987.

(f) Koh-i-Nor Magazine —
'Britain's Allies — the Gurkhas'.

(g) 'Dekho' (Journal of the Burma Star Association) '9th Gurkha Rifles'.

(g) Various articles & papers on Indian Army Subjects, many published.

Broadcasting

(a) TV:
(i) Treasures in Store' — Southern TV on Indian Army Memorial Room, Sandhurst.
(ii) 'Yesterday's Witness — Sahibs' — BBC2.
(iii) CBS News — Harry Reasoner's Column — 'Gurkhas'.
(iv) Thames TV 'For Valour — Prakash Singh' filmed but material used for Brochure.

(b) Radio:
Various interviews on BBC's John Dunn Show, External Services, LBC, and Forces Network in connection with launching of Byron Farwell's Book 'The Gurkhas'.